Alexander L. A. Klauder

**Catholic Practice at Church and at Home**

The parishioners little rule book, a guide for Catholics in the external practice of

their holy religion

Alexander L. A. Klauder

**Catholic Practice at Church and at Home**
The parishioners little rule book, a guide for Catholics in the external practice of their holy religion

ISBN/EAN: 9783337286415

Printed in Europe, USA, Canada, Australia, Japan

Cover: Foto ©Lupo / pixelio.de

More available books at **www.hansebooks.com**

# CATHOLIC PRACTICE
...AT...
## CHURCH AND AT HOME

### The Parishioner's Little Rule Book
A GUIDE FOR CATHOLICS IN THE EX-
TERNAL PRACTICE OF THEIR
HOLY RELIGION

### By REV. ALEXANDER L. A. KLAUDER

*"Let all things be done decently and according to order."*—1 Cor. 14, 40.

*Nihil obstat.*

M. J. BROWN,

*Librorum Censor.*

---

*Imprimatur libellus quem clero et populo enixe commendo.*

✠ HENRICUS,

*Epus Ogdensburgensis.*

# PREFACE.

THIS little book, as its title indicates, is designed to give Catholics some definite rules for the external practice of their holy religion. It is ardently hoped that it will find its way into Catholic families, there to be perused regularly, to be consulted especially when there is doubt about the obligation or manner of performing some duty imposed upon Catholics by the Church. By keeping this little book on hand in some appointed place in the house, and by referring to it on special occasions, such as on feast and fast days, on occasions of a sick-call, baptism, funeral, or other function of religion not so frequent in the family, the faithful will avoid many mistakes, many annoying inconveniences and misunderstandings liable to occur at such times.

We trust the Reverend Clergy will find in these pages the very rules and directions they endeavor so often to impress upon the minds of their parishioners. They may often find it convenient to refer parishioners to this book as containing the written regulations of the parish. Some things here recommended may not harmonize with local custom. Such things may be modified or eliminated according to the exigencies of parish or place. On the other hand there may be important points omitted in this little work through oversight or through an endeavor to make it short and practical. Any suggestion the Reverend Clergy may wish to make to the writer, will be gratefully received.

St. Mary's Cathedral,
Ogdensburg. N. Y., Jan., 1898.

# TABLE OF CONTENTS.

|  | PAGE |
|---|---|
| PREFACE, | v |
| THE PARISH, | 21 |
| BAPTISM, | 23 |
| PRIVATE BAPTISM, | 30 |
| CONFIRMATION, | 33 |
| HOLY EUCHARIST, | 35 |
| HOLY MASS, | 41 |
| POSTURES AND ACTIONS AT HOLY MASS, | 42 |
|     At Low Mass, | 42 |
|     At High Mass, | 43 |
|     At Solemn High Mass, | 44 |
| OTHER ACTIONS AT MASS, | 45 |
| MASS-OFFERINGS, | 47 |
| PUBLIC PRAYERS, | 50 |
| CONGREGATIONAL SINGING, | 51 |
| THE WORD OF GOD, | 52 |
| HOLY COMMUNION, | 56 |
| COMMUNION FOR THE SICK, | 65 |
| FIRST HOLY COMMUNION, | 66 |
| CONFESSION, | 70 |
| EXTREME UNCTION, | 79 |

|  | PAGE |
|---|---|
| SICK CALLS, | 79 |
|     I. Calling the Priest, | 79 |
|     II. Preparation of the Sick Person, | 83 |
|     III. Preparation of the Sick-Room, | 84 |
|     IV. Articles for the Sick-Room, | 86 |
|     V. Administration of the Sacraments, | 88 |
|     VI. After the Administration of the Sacraments, | 91 |
|     VII. Assisting the Dying, | 91 |
| FUNERALS, | 94 |
| MATRIMONY, | 102 |
| THE MARRIAGE-CEREMONY, | 110 |
| THE PRECEPTS OF THE CHURCH, | 119 |
| THE OBLIGATION TO HEAR MASS, | 119 |
| THE HOLYDAYS OF OBLIGATION, | 120 |
| FASTING AND ABSTAINING, | 126 |
|     I. Fasting, | 126 |
|     Fast-Days, | 129 |
|     II. Abstinence, | 130 |
|     Abstinence-Days, | 132 |
| ANNUAL CONFESSION, | 137 |
| THE EASTER DUTY, | 138 |
| SUPPORT OF THE PASTOR AND CHURCH, | 141 |
| THE CLOSED TIME OF MARRIAGE, | 147 |
| RELIGIOUS INSTRUCTION OF CHILDREN, | 148 |
| THE PAROCHIAL SCHOOL, | 153 |
| THE SUNDAY SCHOOL, | 160 |

|                                         | PAGE |
|-----------------------------------------|------|
| RELIGION AT HOME,                       | 164  |
| BLESSINGS AND BLESSED ARTICLES,         | 168  |
| CHURCHING OF WOMEN,                     | 169  |
| BLESSED CANDLES,                        | 171  |
| IMPOSITION OF THE ASHES,                | 172  |
| BLESSED PALM,                           | 173  |
| EASTER WATER,                           | 174  |
| HOLY WATER,                             | 175  |
| ARTICLES OF DEVOTION,                   | 176  |
| THE PRINCIPAL DEVOTIONS,                | 177  |
| VESPERS,                                | 177  |
| BENEDICTION OF THE BLESSED SACRAMENT,   | 178  |
| PLENARY INDULGENCE,                     | 179  |
| THE ROSARY,                             | 182  |
| THE SCAPULAR,                           | 185  |
| THE WAY OF THE CROSS,                   | 188  |
| THE FORTY HOURS' DEVOTION,              | 189  |
| NOVENAS,                                | 191  |
| PIOUS ORGANIZATIONS IN THE PARISH,      | 193  |
| CONDUCT TOWARDS THE PASTOR AND OTHERS OF THE CLERGY, | 201 |

# INDEX.

ABSOLUTION, whilst the Priest imparts, 75; what is to be done when it has been refused, 76; some reasons for the refusal of, 77.

ABSTINENCE, obligation of, 130; days of, 132; who are not obliged to abstain? 131; abstinence from liquor recommended, 131; Abstinence Societies recommended, 200.

ADTIONS AT MASS, 42.

ADDRESSING the clergy, 210.

ADMINISTRATION OF THE SACRAMENTS of the dying, 88.

ADVENT, fast and abstinence days during, 129, 133; hearing of Mass recommended during, 125.

AGNUS DEI, needs no blessing by the Priest, 176.

ALL SAINTS', a holyday of obligation, 120; vigil of, a day of fasting and abstaining, 130, 133.

ALL SOULS' DAY; the hearing of Mass recommended on, 125.

ALTAR-SOCIETY, recommended, 199.

ANGELUS, the recitation of the, in the family to be insisted on, 166.

ANNIVERSARY REQUIEM MASS, having it sung or said each year, 101; when it may be sung, 49.

ANNUAL CONFESSION, 137.

ANOINTING, at baptism, 28; the sick, 90.

ARCHBISHOP, manner of addressing, 211.

ARRANGEMENT OF THE SICK-ROOM, (illustration), 85.

ARTICLES FOR THE SICK-ROOM, 86.

ASCENSION, feast of, a holyday of obligation, 120.
ASHES, blessing and imposition of, 172.
ASSISTING THE DYING, 91.
ASSUMPTION, feast of, a holyday of obligation, 120; vigil of the, a day of fasting and abstinence, 130, 133.

BANS OF MATRIMONY, when to be published, 102; where to be published, 104.
BAPTISM, when to be administered, 23; selecting a name, 24; how the child should be clothed for, 27; how it should be held at, 28; the items for the registration of, 29; private baptism, 30.
BENEDICTION OF THE BLESSED SACRAMENT, 178.
BIBLE, to be kept in every Catholic household, 165; to be read to the family, 167.
BISHOP, conduct toward, 210; manner of addressing, 211.

BLESSINGS AND BLESSED ARTICLES, 168.
BLESSED SACRAMENT. See *Eucharist*.
BOWING, at the mention of the Holy Name, 46; to the Priest when meeting him, 202.
BREAKFAST, in Lent, what custom permits, 127; what kinds of food forbidden at, 127.
BRIDE, rules for, at the marriage-ceremony, 111.
BRIDEGROOM, rules for, at the marriage-ceremony, 111.
BRIDESMAID, rules for, at the marriage-ceremony, 111.
BURIAL, CATHOLIC, who are entitled to, 95; who are excluded from, 95.

CALLING, the Priest to the sick. See *Sick Calls*. Calling on the Priest, 204.
CANDLES, WAX, to be blessed on Candlemas Day, 171; every Catholic household should have, 171; for the sick room, 86; the Priest carry-

ing the Blessed Sacrament to be met at the door with, 88; to be offered at churching, 169; for the decoration of the altar at the Forty Hours' Adoration, 191.
CARDINAL, manner of addressing a, 211.
CATECHISM, to be learned every day, 161; the learning of to be supervised by parents, 149, 161.
CIRCUMCISION of our Lord, a holyday of obligation, 120.
CHILDREN, First Holy Communion of, 66; Instruction of, 148; not to be sent on sick-calls, 79.
CHRISTMAS, a holyday of obligation, 120; Vigil of, a day of fasting and abstaining, 130, 133.
CHURCHING OF WOMEN, 169.
CLERGY, CONDUCT TOWARD THE, 201.
CLOSED TIME OF MARRIAGE, 147.
COFFIN, flowers on, 98; not to be opened in church, 100.
COLLATION, in the evening in Lent, 128.

COMMUNION, Holy, 56; fast necessary for, 56; how to be clothed for, 57; preparation before, 57; how to approach the altar-rail for, 59; the Communion-cloth, 61; how to receive, 63; returning from the Communion-rail, 63; thanksgiving after, 64.
COMMUNION FOR THE SICK, 65; when the sick must receive, 65; the Priest to be notified from time to time, 65.
CONDUCT TOWARD THE PASTOR AND OTHERS OF THE CLERGY, 201.
CONFERENCE OF SAINT VINCENT DE PAUL, recommended, 199.
CONFESSION, 70; Annual, 137; obligation of, 70, 137; knowledge of prayers and points of doctrine necessary for valid reception of, 71; a prayer book to be used in preparing for, 71; the approximate number of mortal sins to be found out, 72; the

confession to be begun promptly, 74.
CONFIRMATION, Sacrament of, 33.
CONGREGATIONAL SINGING, 51.
CONSCIENCE. See *Examination* of.
CONSECRATION, of the Mass, actions and prayers at, 45; what should not be done during, 46.
CONTRITION, act of, to be made before entering the confessional, 73; whilst the Priest pronounces the absolution, 75.
CORPUS CHRISTI, feast of, a day of devotion, 125; the hearing of Mass recommended on it, 125.
CREDO, in the Mass; the faithful to kneel during the, at a Low Mass, 42; to stand and sit during the, at a High Mass, 43.

DAYS OF ABSTINENCE in the United States, 132.
DAYS OF FASTING in the United States, 129.

DEAF PERSONS, not to confess in ordinary confessional, 74.
DEATH, rules to be observed at, 91; immediately after, 94.
DEATH-CHAMBER, rules for, 97.
DEVOTIONS, THE PRINCIPAL, 177.
DYING, ASSISTING THE, 91.

EASTER DUTY, 138; upon whom binding, 138; the time for, 139; the sick must comply with, 139; a particular intention not necessary, 140; not to be put off to the last of the season, 141.
EASTER WATER, 174.
ELEVATION of the Mass. See *Consecration* of the Mass.
EMBER DAYS, 130.
EPIPHANY, feast of, a day of devotion, 125; the hearing of Mass recommended on, 125.
EPISTLE of the Mass; the faithful kneel during, at a Low Mass, 42; sit during, at a High Mass, 43.

EUCHARIST, HOLY, 35; what it is, 35; highest adoration due to, 35; presence of, known by the burning of the sanctuary lamp, 36; reverence due to, when inclosed in tabernacle, 36; when exposed, 37; when carried by the Priest, 39; genuflections to be made to, 36-39.

EXAMINATION OF CONSCIENCE, 72.

EXPOSITION of the Blessed Sacrament. See *Eucharist.*

EXTREME UNCTION, 79; who must receive, 79; what to prepare for, 88; how to assist at, 90.

FAST-DAYS in the United States, 129.

FASTING, 126; what it is, 126; obligation of, 126; who are not obliged to fast, 128.

FIRST HOLY COMMUNION, 66; at what age to be received, 66; previous instruction, 66; duty of parents in regard to which, 67; things necessary for, 68; day of, greatest in the life of a child, 69.

FLOWERS, at funerals, 98; for the decoration of the altar at the Forty Hours' Devotion, 191.

FORTY HOURS' ADORATION, 189.

FUNERALS, 94; prayer at, 96; Funeral Mass, 98; to be on time, 99.

GENUFLECTION, simple, 36; double, 37; how to make a, 39; to be made toward the end of the last gospel, when made by the Priest, 44; when to be made in the sick room, 90.

GLORIA at Mass; the faithful, to kneel during, at a Low Mass, 42; to stand and sit during, at a High Mass, 43.

GLOVES, to be removed before Communion, 57; before entering the sanctuary for matrimony, 111.

GODPARENTS, at baptism, 25; the selection of, 25; the questions they are to answer, 26; rules for their guidance at baptism, 28; spiritual relationship of, 27; duties of, 27; at confirmation, 34.
GROOMSMAN, rules for, at the marriage ceremony, 111.

HAT, to be raised in passing a church, 40; on meeting a Priest, 202.
HIGH MASS, Postures at, 43.
HOLY COMMUNION. See *Communion*.
HOLYDAYS OF OBLIGATION in the United States, 120.
HOLY FAMILY, Archconfraternity of, recommended, 197.
HOLY WATER, 175.
HOLY WEEK, days of abstinence in, 134.

IMMACULATE CONCEPTION, feast of, a holyday of obligation, 120.
IMPEDIMENTS OF MATRIMONY, 104.

IMPOSITION OF THE ASHES, 172.
INDULGENCE. See *Plenary Indulgences*.
INDULTS, permitting the use of flesh-meat, 132, 133.
INTENTIONS for Masses, See *Mass-Offerings*.
INSTRUCTION OF CHILDREN. See *Religious Instruction of Children*.

LATE-COMING to Mass, 123.
LEAGUE OF THE SACRED HEART, recommended, 196.
LETTERS TO THE CLERGY, how to address, 210.
LOW MASS, Postures at, 42.

MARRIAGE-CEREMONY, the, 110; Illustration of, 113; marriage - instruction, 107. See *Matrimony*.
MASS, HOLY, 41; what it is, 41; Postures and Actions at, 42 and 45; obligation to hear, 119; just reasons for omitting, 121; coming late to, 123; hearing

of, on days of devotion recommended, 125.
MASS-OFFERINGS, 47.
MATRIMONY, 102; publication of bans for, 103; impediments of, 104; general confession before, 107; Nuptial Mass and blessing, 108; Words of Third Plenary Council of Baltimore in reference to, 109; ceremony of, 110; questions and answers at, 112; Communion at, 115; thanksgiving after, 116.
MONTH'S MIND; Mass on, recommended, 101; when it may be said, 49.
MYSTERIES OF THE ROSARY, 183.

NATIVITY OF OUR LORD, feast of. See *Christmas*.
NOVENA, what it is and how to make it, 191.
NUPTIAL BLESSING and Nuptial Mass, 108.

OFFERINGS for Masses. See *Mass-Offerings*.
OFFERTORY of the Mass; the faithful to kneel during, at a Low Mass, 42; to sit during, at High Mass, 43.

PALMS, BLESSED, 173.
PARISH, 21.
PAROCHIAL SCHOOL; must be maintained, 153; Decree of the Third Plenary Council of Baltimore regarding, 153; rules for parents regarding, 154-159.
PASTOR, CONDUCT TOWARD THE, 201-211.
PENANCE, Sacrament of. See *Confession*
PEW-RENT, 144.
PLENARY INDULGENCE, 179.
POSTURES at Mass, 42.
PRAYERS of the Mass, the faithful kneel during, at a Low Mass, 42; stand during, at a High Mass, except at Requiem Masses, 43; Public, 50; at the house of mourning, 96; morning and evening, 166; for the intention of the Sovereign Pontiff, 181.
PRECEPTS OF THE CHURCH, 119.

PREFACE of the Mass, the faithful should kneel during, at a Low Mass, 42; stand during, at a High Mass, 43.
PREPARATION before Communion, 57; of a sick person, 83; of the sick-room, 84 and 85.
PRIEST; conduct toward, 201; manner of addressing, 210.
PRIVATE BAPTISM, 30.
PUBLIC PRAYERS, 50.

RELIGION AT HOME, 164.
RELIGIOUS INSTRUCTION OF CHILDREN, 148; duty of parents in regard to, before the children go to school, 148; when they have not the advantage of a parochial, or a Sunday school, 149; parents must bring their children to church with them, 150.
REQUIEM MASSES, 49.
ROSARY, 182.

SCAPULAR, 185.
SICK-CALLS, 79.

SICK-ROOM, PREPARATION OF THE. 84; ARRANGEMENT OF THE, (Illustration,) 85.
SODALITY, OF THE CHILDREN OF MARY, recommended, 198; OF THE LIVING ROSARY, 198.
SOLEMN HIGH MASS, 44.
SPONSORS. See *Godparents*.
STATIONS OF THE CROSS. See *Way of the Cross*.
STIPENDS. See *Mass-Offerings*.
SUNDAY SCHOOL, 160; who must attend, 160; rules for parents regarding, 160.
SUPPORT OF PASTOR, 141; who are bound by this precept, 142; duty to support the parochial school, 145; Decree of Third Plenary Council of Baltimore concerning, 145.

TABLE for the sick-room, 86; Illustration of the, 87.
TABLE OF SINS, in using the, 72.
TEMPERANCE-SOCIETIES, recommended, 200.

THANKSGIVING after Communion, 64.
THINGS FOR THE SICK-ROOM. See *Articles for the Sick-Room.*
TITLES to be given to the Clergy, 210.
THIRD ORDER OF SAINT FRANCIS, recommended, 196.

UNDERTAKER, Catholic, to be employed, 94.

VESPERS, 177.
VIATICUM; no necessity to fast before, 84.

VIGILS of feasts, as days of abstinence, 133.
VISITING the Priest, 204; the teacher at school, 155, 156.

WAKE, 96.
WATER, Holy. See *Holy Water.*
Easter Water. See *Easter-Water.* At private baptism, 31.
WAY OF THE CROSS, 188.
WAX CANDLES. See *Candles.*
WHITSUNDAY, Vigil of, a day of fasting and abstaining, 130 and 133.
WOMEN, Churching of, 169.
WORD OF GOD, 52.

## THE PARISH.

As a Catholic, you are, ordinarily, a member of a certain parish, which in this country is a designated district or class of persons assigned by the Bishop to a church and to the spiritual care of a Pastor.

When moving into a new locality, let it be your first duty to inquire for your parish church.

Introduce yourself to the Reverend Pastor as soon as possible. If you are the head of the family, or are in charge of a household, be ready to give the Pastor the names of all its members, together with their ages and their condition in life, that he may be enabled at once to enter all the names on the parish register. You will thereby enable both him and yourself to know your mutual obligations and save yourselves possible inconveniences, which often arise in parishes through the presence of families unknown to the Pastor. The latter will then also be able the better to attend to your wants, to visit you, especially at the time of his regular visitations.

On moving out of a parish, be sure to advise the Reverend Pastor of it, so that your name may be crossed off the parish books and many inconveniences and misunderstandings be thereby avoided. Both religious conscientiousness and common gratitude ought to dictate such a course.

If new Catholic neighbors move into the parish, who are not likely to make themselves known to the Pastor, it will be charity on your part to remind them of that obligation, or to inform the Pastor yourself of their arrival.

Should you merely change your residence in the parish, you should likewise give notice to the Pastor that he may note the change and spare himself and his co-laborers possible inconveniences.

Should there be several parishes, as is sometimes the case in this country, covering the same territory, in favor of various languages, remember that you are bound to adhere to the one to which you have been assigned, or which you have selected yourself, according to existing regulations. To go now to one and then to another for various purposes, merely to enjoy a personal advantage in the one and to escape a burden in the other, is unjust, productive of confusion, and renders one liable to be overlooked in the hour of need, with no one to blame but oneself.

## BAPTISM.

A newly born child should be baptized as soon as possible. To put off the sacrament for three or four weeks, and even longer, without very grave reasons, may be a grievous sin.

In most parishes there is an hour appointed for baptism, usually on Sunday afternoon. Have the child brought to the church on the first occasion of the kind.

If sickness of the child, great distance, intense cold, or other excusing circumstances should exist, notify the Pastor of the same at once, and abide by his arrangements. By no means take the matter wholly into your own hands and thereby defer baptism.

In selecting a name for the child, regard should be had to the wish of the Church that the name of a saint or holy person, either of the New or Old Law, be adopted. If a family-name be given, the name of some saint should at least accompany it. Where this has not been done, the name of a saint may be added at confirmation.

When the hour for baptism is, or has been specially appointed, be sure to be on time. Urge the Godparents particularly on this point. The Priest has on Sundays, as well as on other days, his appointments, services and engagements, in all of which he must be prompt. If parties should come late and have to be put off to another time, let them blame themselves.

Select Godparents, or sponsors, as they are also called, who are good, practical Catholics, who are well instructed in the faith and are able to bring up a child in the same. Let them, therefore, be neither too young nor too old, as they must assume the spiritual care of the child in case the parents of it should die, or should neglect it.

Non-Catholics are not permitted by the laws of the Church to be Godparents; neither are apostate Catholics, nor members of secret societies specially condemned by the Church.

If two Godparents, or sponsors are engaged, they must be of different sexes. Employing two Godfathers or two Godmothers is not permissible. If one Godparent is employed, it may be either Godfather or Godmother.

Godparents should be prepared to answer the following questions, which the Priest asks them during the ceremony of baptism.

*Priest.* *N.* What dost thou ask of the Church of God?

*Godparents.* Faith.

*Priest.* What doth faith bring thee to?

*Godparents.* Life everlasting.

*Priest. N.* Dost thou renounce Satan?

*Godparents.* I do renounce him.

*Priest.* And all his works?

*Godparents.* I do renounce them.

*Priest.* And all his pomps?

*Godparents.* I do renounce them.

*Priest. N.* Dost thou believe in God the Father Almighty, Creator of heaven and earth?

*Godparents.* I do believe.

*Priest.* Dost thou believe in Jesus Christ, His only Son our Lord, Who was born into this world and Who suffered for us?

*Godparents.* I do believe.

*Priest.* Dost thou believe in the Holy Ghost, the Holy Catholic Church, the Communion of Saints, the forgiveness of sins, the resurrection of the body, and life everlasting?

*Godparents.* I do believe.

*Priest. N.* Wilt thou be baptized?

*Godparents.* I will.

The Godparents will be called upon to recite the Apostles' Creed aloud. Let them, therefore, know it well by heart.

Let Godparents not forget the obligation they take upon themselves in standing for a child, to care for its Christian training and instruction, especially in the case of the death of the parents or of neglect on their part.

Let them also remember that they contract a spiritual relationship with their Godchild, as well as with its parents, so that they can never marry anyone of the said parties.

See Impediments of Matrimony, Page 104.

The clothing about the neck of the child

should be so arranged that it may be easily loosened, as the Priest must anoint the breast of the child and the back between the shoulders. Do not keep your fingers over these parts in forcing back the clothing, lest they get touched with the holy oil. Have the clothing loose and there will be no trouble.

In holding the infant during the ceremonies, have its head uncovered and let it rest, face upward, on the right arm.

Whilst the Priest pours the water on the head, if there be two Godparents, let one place his right hand on or under the right shoulder of the child, whilst the other holds it, as both Godparents must touch the child during the baptizing.

Hold the crown of the head, face downward, exactly over the middle of the baptismal bowl or basin, almost on a level with it. Support the head with the right hand spread under the neck or chin of the child.

After the priest has poured the water, he dries the head, which should be kept over the bowl during the time. He then anoints the crown of the head with holy Chrism.

There must be **no talking, smiling** or **making of remarks** during the sacred ceremony of baptism, but all attendants must stand by with the profoundest reverence and respect, as they would at any other service in the church.

Those who bring a child or accompany a person to be baptized, must be prepared to supply the following items for the correct registering of the baptism: The exact date of the child or person's birth, the place of birth, the full names of the father of the child and his place of birth, town, city or county, and country; the mother's full names, her maiden or family-name before marriage, together with the exact place of her birth; the full names of the Godparents.

Let parents or Godparents, or both, according to the custom of the parish, make an offering to the Priest. In case of poverty or temporary inability, let them have an understanding with the Priest beforehand. Baptism must never be deferred on account of inability to make such an offering.

## PRIVATE BAPTISM.

Try to read these rules before administering private baptism, if there is time.

If an unbaptized child, or person who desires to be baptized, is in danger of death, and it is convenient to call the Priest, he should be summoned without delay.

But if there is danger of such a child or person dying before the priest can reach them, let any one present who has the use of reason, administer baptism.

The parents themselves, however, ought not to do it, if any one else present is able to do so.

To baptize privately simply follow these instructions: Take common water from the faucet or well, or wherever you can get it. Don't bother about holy water, Easter water or any other particular kind of water; take common water.

Pour this water on the head of the child or person; don't merely sprinkle it with your fingers; but pour it from some vessel, parting the hair if it is thick, with one hand, so that the water will touch the skin of the top of the head, or forehead at least.

Whilst pouring the water say these words and no others: **I baptize thee in the name of the Father and of the Son and of the Holy Ghost.** Be sure to say the words: **I baptize thee**, and not merely the words: In the name of the Father and of the Son and of the Holy Ghost.

Don't bother about making the sign of the cross, but only pour the water over the head, saying the above-mentioned words.

Don't be concerned about a name for the child or about the selection of a Godparent. All that is unnecessary at a private baptism. Lose no time.

If a child baptized at home, whether by Priest or by lay-person, should recover, it must, nevertheless, be brought to the church, as though it had not been baptized at all; so that the priest may supply the prayers and ceremonies prescribed at baptisms in church. A Godparent must stand for it then, and a name must be given to it.

When such a child is brought to church, the fact of private baptism must be mentioned to the Priest at once before he begins the ceremonies of baptism, so that he may know exactly which prayers and functions he is to perform and which he is to omit.

The Priest does not baptize such a child again, if it has been properly baptized at home, but has only to supply the remaining ceremonies and prayers.

Let the one who baptized such a child privately, if possible, accompany it to the church, so that the Priest may ascertain whether the child had been validly baptized or not.

See that the private baptism of a child is duly recorded by the Priest in the parish records of baptism, whether the child survive or not.

## CONFIRMATION.

EVERY Catholic having attained the age of reason, is obliged to receive the holy sacrament of confirmation under pain of sin.

Those who have neglected it after their twelfth year or thereabouts, or may never have had the opportunity to receive it, are obliged under pain of grievous sin to prepare themselves for its reception, when an occasion presents itself, no matter how old they may be.

Hence, such must make themselves known to the Pastor, so that he may advise them when the first opportunity arrives, and have them duly instructed and prepared.

To receive this sacrament worthily a Catholic must be sufficiently instructed in his holy religion and concerning the character and purpose of this sacrament. He must, moreover, be in the state of grace when he receives it. Hence the custom of previously going to confession.

It is not, however, necessary to receive Holy Communion on the day of confirmation, although it is customary to do so.

Unless the Pastor has provided, the candidates for confirmation must have a Godfather or Godmother, commonly called a sponsor, according to the sex of the candidate, who contracts a spiritual relationship with the candidate, the same as a Godparent at baptism.

See Impediments of Matrimony, Page 104.

The name of a saint is usually given the candidate at confirmation, which should be carefully selected by the candidate beforehand.

No one must approach the Bishop for confirmation unless by the previous consent of the Pastor or Priest in charge of those to be confirmed, nor without a card for the purpose, bearing the name under which the candidate is to be confirmed.

## THE HOLY EUCHARIST.

THE Holy Eucharist is the sacrament which contains the body and blood, soul and divinity of our Lord Jesus Christ under the appearances of bread and wine.

As the Holy Eucharist or Blessed Sacrament contains our Blessed Saviour Himself, it must receive the highest adoration as to God Himself.

The presence of the Blessed Sacrament in church is known by the burning of the sanctuary-lamp before the altar on which the Blessed Sacrament is kept in the tabernacle. Sometimes the lamp may be on the altar itself, or at least close to it.

The Blessed Sacrament is kept in the tabernacle under the form of bread, in the sacred host.

Every Catholic passing in or out of a church, or before an altar, containing the Blessed Sacrament, must bend the knee, and at all times observe the profoundest respect and silence whilst the Blessed Eucharist is present.

When the Blessed Sacrament is inclosed in the tabernacle or is not in immediate sight, as at Holy Mass, the bending of the knee, or genuflecting, as it is commonly called, is done with the right knee only, bending it down to the floor. The genuflection with one knee is called a simple genuflection.

When the Blessed Sacrament is exposed, however, to general view, as at Benediction, at the Exposition during the Forty Hours' Devotion, or on other occasions, or when a person is passing before a Priest who is distributing Holy Communion, the genuflection must be made with both knees with an inclination of the head at the same time. People, however, who are themselves receiving Holy Communion, need not make more than a simple genuflection on coming to the Communion-rail, or on leaving it. The genuflection made with both knees is called a double or profound genuflection.

On entering a church where the Blessed Sacrament is kept, it is customary not to make the genuflection until one enters the pew or arrives at the place where one intends to remain.

On leaving the church the genuflection is made at the nearest point where one is leaving the presence of the Blessed Sacrament, as at the exit of the pew, or at the altar-rail, side chapel or other point of departure.

Do not make a genuflection immediately on entering or leaving the church inside of the door, which is superfluous and awkward, especially when there are crowds entering or leaving.

Do not genuflect on leaving the pew when you are going to the altar, but wait until you have come before the altar. In like manner do not genuflect before the pew when you have returned from the altar-rail, but make your genuflection at the latter place only.

In crossing from one side of the church to the other, whether in the front, middle or rear of the church, a genuflection must always be made toward the altar where the Blessed Sacrament is kept or exposed.

A genuflection must likewise be made to the altar of the Blessed Sacrament in passing it by the side, or in the rear of it, as in going from the body of the church into the vestry or sacristy.

In making a genuflection, one should be careful to make it properly, that is, to bend the knee all the way to the floor, and not to support oneself on a pew or other object. Awkwardness in this respect is excusable only in persons stiff with age or disease. In all others it is carelessness and irreverence.

When the priest carries the Blessed Sacrament from one place to another, in procession, or to the sick, everyone should fall on his knees and remain in that position until the priest has passed out of sight, or put the Blessed Sacrament back into its place of keeping.

On entering or leaving the church the greatest care must be taken not to make any noise, as by hard and rapid walking, slamming doors and the like. The church is the holiest place on earth, and not less holy than heaven itself, for God is really present in both places. "The place whereon thou standest is holy." Jos. 5. 16.

When others enter the pew in which you are, move down, so as to compel no one to climb over you; or if you wish to remain at the entrance of the pew, rise, get out into the aisle, and step back, so as to let the new-comer pass in before you.

In passing before the church, men and boys should always raise their hats, in honor of the Blessed Sacrament, whether walking or riding. This is a distinct profession of faith, and non-Catholics always expect to see it in Catholics. Women should bow the head, bless themselves, or make some other act of reverence.

In passing in the immediate vicinity of the church, and especially if the door or windows should be open, no one should raise his voice so as to be heard in the church.

Standing and holding conversation in the parts adjoining the church, such as in the porch of the church and in the passages, is a great abuse of the sacred edifice of God.

## HOLY MASS.

THE Mass is the unbloody sacrifice of the Body and Blood of Christ. It is the highest act of divine worship in the Catholic Church.

The principal actions of the Mass are the offering of bread and wine, the changing of them into the Body and Blood of Christ, and the consuming or receiving of them.

Every Catholic who can read, should familiarize himself with the parts of the Mass, and with the various prayers and devotions at the same by the constant use of prayer-books. Every one should likewise, but especially those who cannot read, provide himself with rosary-beads.

The most appropriate prayer-book at Mass is the one that corresponds to the Mass-book or missal on the altar, from which it is translated, which can be had from any Catholic publisher. But all prayer-books contain appropriate Mass-devotions.

## Postures and Actions at Holy Mass.

Try to be as near to the altar during Mass as possible. Do not remain in the rear of the church when there is room in the front. The idea of assisting at Mass is to be as near to the altar of sacrifice, to join in the service and to follow it as closely as possible.

**At Low Mass.** At Low Mass all should kneel during the whole Mass, standing only at the gospels. In some places the faithful stand also during the Credo, if it is said, which is immediately after the first gospel. They bend the knee with the Priest at the words, "*Et homo factus est.*"

If anyone wishes to sit during the Mass, especially if he is not able to kneel during the whole time, he may sit down after the Credo until the Sanctus-bell is rung. Another time suitable for sitting is after the Communion, whilst the Priest purifies and covers the chalice, until he begins to read the last prayers.

**At High Mass.** All stand during the sprinkling of the congregation before the Mass. They kneel at the Mass until the Priest intones the Gloria, when they stand. They sit whenever the Priest sits, whilst the announcements are made and during the sermon. They stand during the singing of the prayers; except at a Requiem Mass. They sit during the reading of the Epistle until the book is carried over. They stand at the Gospel, also at the Credo, whilst the Priest is standing. They sit at the Credo when the Priest sits, kneeling down when the Choir sings the passage, "*Et incarnatus est,*" rising after the words, "*Et homo factus est.*" They sit during the Offertory and rise when the Priest sings the *Per omnia* *sacula saculorum* for the Preface. They kneel from the Sanctus until after the Communion. They sit whilst the Priest purifies and covers the chalice. They stand during the last prayers, kneel for the blessing, and stand during the last Gospel.

When the Priest says the words, "*And the Word was made Flesh,*" toward the end of the Gospel, and genuflects, the faithful should genuflect likewise, and rise again with him. Some people remain kneeling at that point of the Gospel, which is not correct.

No one should leave the church before the Priest has left the sanctuary.

**At Solemn High Mass.** A High Mass is called solemn, when at least three sacred ministers officiate, that is the Celebrant, a Deacon and a Subdeacon. The same postures are observed as at High Mass. The faithful, however, should stand not whilst the first Gospel is being read by the celebrant, at the altar, but whilst it is being sung immediately after by the deacon.

They should stand also when the altar-boy incenses the congregation.

## Other Actions at Holy Mass.

IT is a pious custom to bow low and strike the breast at the ringing of the bell during the Consecration and at the Communion.

Whilst striking the breast at the Consecration we might say, " Jesus, for Thee will I live; Jesus, for Thee will I die; Jesus, Thine will I be in life and in death ;" or, " Jesus, I believe in Thee; Jesus, I hope in Thee; Jesus, I love Thee with all my heart."

Whilst striking the breast at Communion we should say three times, " Lord, I am not worthy that Thou shouldst enter under my roof; but only say the word, and my soul shall be healed."

To strike the breast properly, lay the left hand a little below it and strike it with the thumb and first two fingers of the right hand.

At the beginning of the Gospels, lay your left hand on your breast and with the thumb of your right hand, spreading at the same time your other fingers, make a small cross on your forehead, on your lips and on your breast.

Always bow the head at the mention of the Sacred Name of Jesus, whether during the Mass or during the sermon. Do not forget this. All devout Catholics do it.

Bow the head also whilst the "Gloria Patri," or "Glory be to the Father," is being said or sung at any service, and when the Priest gives the blessing.

Do not walk in the church, in the vestry, or parts adjoining the sanctuary, speak, or perform any service except that connected with another Mass, whilst the Consecration of a Mass is going on. At the sound of the bell everyone should fall on his knees, in whatever place about the church he may be, and assist in profound adoration.

The same rule should be observed also whenever a priest gives out Holy Communion. All in and about the church should kneel and assist at it. If there should be a large number of communicants, all should remain kneeling at least until the priest begins to administer Communion at the rail.

## MASS-OFFERINGS.

As the special fruit of the Holy Sacrifice of the Mass accrues to those to whom the latter is particularly applied, it is customary for the faithful to make a special offering to the Priest for this purpose. This offering is also called a stipend.

The usual offering or stipend for a Low Mass is one dollar; for a High Mass, different sums, according as they are fixed in different localities and according to the character of the High Mass. The Priest is not at liberty to change these rates.

The offering should invariably be given in advance. This should not be considered a matter of business on the part of the Priest, so much as a matter of conscientiousness and religious propriety on the part of the petitioner for the special fruit of the Mass, whom custom requires to make an actual offering in connection with the Mass. It does not seem proper to make the offering after the Mass is over.

In the case of poor people who cannot afford to make an offering for a Mass, not even in favor of a deceased relative at the time of death, the Priest may donate the Mass; in which case he makes the offering himself, or sacrifices that which is otherwise his due, in favor of another.

Persons wishing to have a Mass said or sung on a certain date, should make the arrangements together with the offering some time in advance.

As High Masses usually take the precedence of Low Masses and require more special arrangements, these should be made even sooner in advance.

In having Low Masses said, one should not insist too much on the time and place for their celebration, as the Priest cannot usually bind himself in that way.

Masses for the Dead in black vestments can be said only on certain days; hence, one dare not insist too much on their being said on a particular date.

A Requiem Mass for the Third Day, Seventh Day, or Thirtieth Day after death, or Month's Mind, as the latter is called, as well as for an Anniversary, which cannot be said on the proper date in deference to the rules of the Church, requiring the Mass of the feast-day to be celebrated only; may, however, be said on the first day after such date not impeded by the rules of the Church. Parties insisting on such

Masses being said on the date proper, or wishing to have other Masses for the dead said on a day not open to them by the rules of the Church, must be satisfied to have the Masses said in vestments of the color appointed for that day.

## PUBLIC PRAYERS.

It is a matter for regret that in many churches the public prayers on the part of the congregation amount to nothing more than an unintelligible murmuring.

All should answer loudly and distinctly, so that each one may plainly hear his own words.

Where it is customary to make certain pauses in the recitation of the prayers, each one should endeavor to observe them, so as not to get ahead of others.

No one should begin his part before the Priest or leader has finished his.

In the recitation of the litanies and of other devotions each one should use a prayer-book until he becomes familiar with the exact answers to the various invocations.

## CONGREGATIONAL SINGING.

EVERY member of the congregation possessing a good voice ought to join the choir, or ought at least to join in the singing of the ordinary responses at Mass, where it is customary, as well as of the hymns sung in the vernacular.

The choir ought to be scrupulous in rendering the correct responses to the singing of the Priest and not neglect them as of little importance, devoting most of their attention principally to the rendition of grand compositions.

When an English hymn is sung, let each member of the congregation look for it in his prayer-book and endeavor to join in.

It is the earnest desire of the heads of the Church that congregational singing be introduced everywhere. The children are taught it in school and in Sunday school, but, strange to say, do not, as a rule, continue the practice after they leave school, when they kneel in the congregation at large.

## THE WORD OF GOD.

CATHOLICS are bound under pain of sin to hear the word of God preached by the Priest.

Hence, those who always go to a Low Mass on Sunday, at which the word of God is not preached, and avoid the principal Mass on account of the sermon, are guilty of sin.

There is usually a five-minute sermon, however, preached at the Low Masses. This is in favor of those who are not able to attend the High Mass either on that particular Sunday, or regularly, through their peculiar occupations; but this short sermon is not intended to supply the average Catholic with the word of God throughout the year. Hence the obligation to attend also the High Mass and principal sermon of the Sunday from time to time.

Some are fond of a good sermon, but do not care for plain instructions. The latter, as a rule, are more necessary for most Catholics than eloquent sermons.

The Pastor is bound under pain of sin to give such instructions, both in favor of those who have not yet heard them, as well as for others, in order to keep the doctrines and practices of religion fresh in the minds of the faithful. Hence all parishioners should attend them, whether they are familiar with them or not.

Some attend sermons only when preached by this or that Priest whom they are fond of hearing, but neglect the word of God on other occasions. This is wrong. We should hear the word of God regularly as a duty, independently of the preacher.

Some Catholics do not like to attend sermons because they always seem dry and old to them. They always want to hear something new. They forget, however, that God, truth, religion, heaven and hell remain always the same; that the same sins are always being committed, and that the same remedies must be applied. They should not forget that the poor Priest's life is always more or less the same on their account. Indeed, is not the life of the average Christian in its everyday duties more or less always the same? Such Christians, tired of the ordinary sermons, and desiring always new and sensational ones, are liable to be the very people who are responsible for sameness in sermons. They are generally Christians of the most monotonous and stereotyped character. They never make a change in their prayers and devotions, always commit and confess the same sins and make no progress in virtue whatever. Yet, they would have the priest always to give them something new. It is usually the lukewarm who complain of the dryness of sermons. The devout Catholic always loves to hear the word of God; and he usually finds something new in it as often as it is preached to him. The trouble is not so much with the sermons, as with the hearers.

The late Mass, usually a High Mass with sermon, should always be attended by one or more members of the family. It is well for the members of the household to go to the different Masses in turn, unless an employment obliges one always to go to the same Mass.

Those who cannot come to church to hear the word of God, must try to read it at home in the Sacred Scriptures and in other religious books.

## HOLY COMMUNION.

To receive Holy Communion a strict fast from midnight on is necessary, so that absolutely nothing be taken in the shape of food or drink, not even medicine.

As to the fast of the sick, see article, Communion for the Sick, Page 65.

Water taken into the mouth, but not perceptibly swallowed, does not break this fast, such as in rinsing the mouth, brushing the teeth and the like.

In case of doubt about having broken the fast, consult a Priest about it before attempting to receive.

There is no obligation to go to Holy Communion after one has gone to confession, unless it should be one's Easter Duty, and there should be no other occasion to comply with it. One may go to confession at any time without going to Holy Communion.

Make a special effort to dress well when you receive Holy Communion. The dignity of the sacrament demands it. Let men and boys always attend particularly to their neck-dress and to their shoes. To receive Holy Communion without a collar, or with a soiled one, is unpardonable slovenliness and irreverence; and to approach the Holy Table with soiled shoes, unless it be on a very rainy morning or at a season of unusual mud or dust, is an equal sign of great disrespect.

It is not proper to wear gloves at the Communion-rail.

Never go to church to receive Holy Communion without a prayer-book and prayer-beads, at least a prayer-book; or beads, if you cannot read.

Do not approach the altar-rail without having prayed at least a quarter of an hour, as an immediate preparation.

If Holy Communion should be distributed before Mass for the convenience of a few, do not receive then, if you can wait until the Communion-time of the Mass; and never approach the holy table without having prepared yourself by at least a quarter of an hour's prayer.

Those who go to Communion but once or a few times in the year, should not easily go on a week day, if they must hurry on account of their work, and when they can go on Sunday just as well. Such are scarcely able to receive Holy Communion properly on a week-day morning.

When intending to receive Holy Communion take your position in church as near to the altar as pew-regulations and the crowd will permit.

Approach the altar immediately after the bell has been rung for the Priest's Communion; or if you receive outside of the Mass, as soon as the signal has been given and the server recites the Confiteor.

Do not bend the knee on leaving the pew, but when you have arrived at the rail; then rise and kneel close up to the rail. Where there are several steps, however, leading to the rail, it is well to kneel on the lowest step until the Priest descends from the platform of the altar.

Fold your hands before your breast in going to and from the rail, and do not let them hang by your sides. Cast your eyes down and do not look about.

Try to kneel at the middle of the rail immediately before the main altar, unless other communicants have already taken up that place. Never kneel toward the end of the rail, if the middle of the rail is free; in which latter case walk to the middle of the rail and do not oblige the Priest to carry the Blessed Sacrament all the way to you at the other end of the rail, or farther from the main altar than is necessary. If your seat is in the side aisle, let it not prevent you from going to the middle of the rail. Let your endeavor be always to receive Holy Communion directly before the main altar, when possible, whether there be many communicants or few. In some large churches no attention is paid to those who kneel at the end of the rail when the middle of it is free. Often the Priest cannot tell who has received, and who has not, especially when the church is large and there are many communicants coming and going. Sometimes a pulpit or pillar obstructs his view.

Make the sign of the cross on yourself when the Priest turns toward the people pronouncing the absolution after the Confiteor.

Strike your breast three times when he holds up the Saced Host turned toward you and says three times the "*Domine non sum dignus.*" Say likewise each time as you strike your breast the same words in English, "Lord, I am not worthy that thou shouldst enter under my roof; but only say the word, and my soul shall be healed."

If it is a cloth you hold over your hands —for the communicant must always be provided with some kind of cloth or spread to hold before the breast—be sure to stretch out the palms of your hands perfectly flat, that the cloth may be flattened out before your chin in the manner of a small table-spread, so that, in case the Holy Communion should be accidentally dropped, it may not fall to the floor. To hold the cloth in a pointed manner over the folded hands does not altogether answer the purpose for which it is intended.

In returning from the rail, do not drop the cloth to the floor, if there are others to receive; but try to keep it spread over the rail.

If the cloth should not be raised over the rail when you are about to receive, reach for it and adjust it for yourself. Never attempt to receive without the requisite cloth or substitute for the same.

If a card is used for the communicants instead of a cloth, be sure you pass it to your neighbor after you have received, if there is no altar-boy to take it from you.

When there is more than one railing of communicants, retire at once when you have received. Make a simple genuflection on the floor before the rail at the place where you have received, and return to your pew without making another genuflection.

Do not approach to receive Holy Communion if you are feeling sick at the stomach. If an accident should happen after receiving, or you greatly fear one, you should go to the vestry and make it known to the Priest or to some one in charge.

Avoid spitting and expectorating for at least a quarter of an hour after Holy Communion.

Remember it is not permitted to touch the Sacred Host with the fingers. If it should cleave to any part of the mouth, loosen it gradually with the tongue and swallow it.

Try to swallow the Sacred Host as soon as possible. Do not think that you ought to let it melt in your mouth.

In the act of receiving hold your face up, but do not look into the face of the Priest or in any direction. Keep your eyes cast down.

Put out your tongue so as to let it cover the lower lip entirely.

Practice these last rules occasionally at home before going to Holy Communion. Frequent communicants sometimes get into habits of carelessness in these matters.

If there have been only a few communicants at Mass or you have been among the last ones to receive, remain at the railing until the Priest has returned to the altar and has closed the door of the tabernacle.

When Holy Communion is distributed outside of Mass and there have been but a few communicants, they, or the last ones that have received, if there have been many, should remain at the altar-rail until the Priest has given the blessing, except before or after a Requiem Mass, when he omits the blessing.

Do not leave the church a few minutes after you have received. Always remain at least a quarter of an hour in thanksgiving after Holy Communion.

Do not leave the church, as a rule, immediately after the Mass when you have received at the regular time. It is seldom a quarter of an hour from Communion-time until the end of the Mass, unless there has been an unusually large number of communicants, and you have been among the first to receive. To leave immediately after Mass when one has received but a few minutes before, looks very bad, shows ignorance, thoughtlessness and irreverence in religious matters.

If you are entitled to a plenary indulgence by receiving Holy Communion, do not forget to say some special prayers for the intention of the Holy Father, to the extent at least of five times the Our Father and Hail Mary.

## COMMUNION FOR THE SICK.

SICK people, invalids and such as cannot come to church to receive Holy Communion, although in no danger of death, must, nevertheless, receive from time to time at their homes, or at least during the Easter time.

See Fourth Precept of the Church, The Easter Duty, Page 138.

Notify the Priest about such persons and abide by his instructions. If he should promise to bring Communion at stated intervals, be sure to remind him in advance each time, and arrange with him the exact day and hour of his coming.

Do not fix the time yourself and then send him word. Do not make the arrangements through another Priest or through any one else. The Priest who carries Holy Communion must make the arrangements in person with the parties responsible for the sick person. Do not expect him to bring Communion on a Sunday, feast-day or other occasion when he is very much occupied in the church.

As for the preparation necessary for the Communion of the Sick, see article, Sick Calls, Page 79.

## FIRST HOLY COMMUNION.

When children have arrived at their twelfth year, as a rule, or even earlier than that, according to the custom of the country, their parents are bound in conscience to see that they be prepared to receive their first Holy Communion.

If such a child should be unknown to the Pastor or be overlooked by those in charge, the parents themselves must notify the former.

There is a course of special instructions given in the parish usually about three months in advance of the first Holy Communion of the children.

Parents are bound to see that their children who are of age to receive their first Holy Communion, attend these instructions regularly, or in case of positive inability to do so, make the excuse known to the Pastor and abide by his instructions.

Parents are, moreover, bound to make sure during this time, and especially as the Communion-day approaches, that their children give satisfaction at the instructions, otherwise they might be suddenly dropped from the roll and put back to the next year. Let them go to the Pastor occasionally and make inquiries.

The parents must also employ special care that their children make efforts during this time to lay aside such faults and habits to which they may have been addicted in the past; such as going with bad companions, sinful language, grave acts of disobedience, neglect of prayer and of their religious duties, and the like.

When special religious exercises are held for the children a few days before their first Holy Communion, parents must by no means permit them to miss these exercises by employing them at home, sending them on errands, permitting them to go to amusements and for similar reasons.

The children should be clothed for the occasion according to the regulations of the parish. Parents too poor to provide the outfit, should report to the Pastor, but by no means keep a child from Holy Communion through poverty.

On the other hand, parents should not make a display of their children on the day of their first Holy Communion by dressing them more stylishly than other children, allowing them the use of special jewelry and the like.

Every child should be provided with a new child's prayer-book and a new pair of beads for that occasion. Other presents may be given it on its first Communion day after it has received, but not to make a display of them on that day.

Candles, flowers and the articles prescribed by the Pastor should be cheerfully provided and should be in accordance with the regulations.

Parents should not forget that the day of first Holy Communion is the greatest in the life of a child, and no expense, pains and preparation can be too great for that important occasion.

Children should not be permitted to go to amusements the day before their first Holy Communion or on the day itself. They should be sent to bed early on the eve, given a light, warm and strengthening supper and made to abstain from cold drinks and fresh fruits and vegetables. The latter tend to sicken a child not yet accustomed to fasting.

The day of the first Holy Communion should not be made the occasion of carousing and the holding of parties and amusements, but a day given entirely to piety and to the religious exercises in the church.

Where customary, let parents cheerfully make the usual offering to the Priest or to the instructors of their children for the great pains they had taken in the performance of such an important and arduous task.

## CONFESSION.

It is a commandment of the Church that all Catholics having the use of reason, confess their sins at least once in the year.

Hence, when children get to be about seven years of age, they must be instructed and prepared to make a confession.

It is the duty of parents to arrange with the Priest concerning this matter, unless they know positively that he has already attended to it.

In sending a child to confession, see that it knows the principal prayers of our holy religion, the Our Father, Hail Mary, and the Apostles' Creed, together with the Confiteor and the Act of Contrition, to be found in the catechism and in most prayer-books.

To receive the sacrament of penance validly every Christian must know also the principal truths of our holy religion, the existence of God, of the Most Blessed Trinity, of Redemption by Christ, and of the reward and punishment of sin.

**Use a prayer-book** in preparing yourself as well as others for confession. In this way we gradually learn which sins are committed against the different commandments of God and of the Church, as well as other kinds of sins, and how to confess them. If you can read, therefore, never approach the sacrament of penance without a prayer-book, unless long use of the same and frequent reception of the sacraments have made you very familiar with the prayers and forms connected with the sacraments.

Never permit your children to go to confession without a prayer-book.

Spend some time in church before going into the confessional in prayer and in examining your conscience. Use a prayer-book for the same.

In examining your conscience according to the printed table of sins to be found in the prayer-book, or according to some other method, be sure to find out also by sufficient reflection the number of times you may have committed any mortal sin.

If you cannot find out the exact number of times, make as close a guess as you can. Say about how often you may have committed the sin since your last worthy confession, either altogether, or in a year, in a month, in a week, or even in a day.

Never tell the confessor that you cannot give the number of times, for everyone can make a rough guess at least.

Never indulge in conversation before the confessional, but keep on examining your conscience if you must wait for your turn, or saying prayers, especially repeating the act of contrition.

Never forget to make an act of contrition before entering the confessional.

When there is a number of penitents of both sexes, and there are at the same time two apartments in the confessional, one for men and the other for women, enter the confessional only on the side assigned to your sex. As soon as it is your turn, enter promptly whilst the Priest is hearing on the other side, so as not to make him lose any time in waiting for you.

Never enter a confessional, however, when a Priest is hearing a confession on the one side, and there is no one else or only a few people in the church. The voices can easily be heard in such a case and much embarrassment may arise for all parties. Both sides of the confessional are to be occupied at the same time, only, when there is a number of penitents and the Priest is pressed for time.

Deaf people and persons hard of hearing generally, must not attempt to make their confession in the ordinary confessional. They must notify the Priest at once that they cannot hear well, that he may take them to the vestry or to some other place appointed for the hearing of deaf people. If there is no particular time or place appointed for the confessions of deaf persons, the latter do well to make special arrangements with the Priest.

The moment the Priest appears, begin your confession. Do not hesitate or wait for the Priest to address you. This is very annoying especially when there is a large crowd of penitents to be heard. Begin your confession at once by asking the Priest's blessing.

Make the Priest ask you as few questions as possible.

When there is a large number of penitents, and you are accustomed to say the long confession-prayer or Confiteor, cut it short; ask the Priest's blessing in a few words, state the time of your last confession and begin to tell your sins. Some say the confession-prayer whilst they are waiting their turn in the confessional.

If you have not received absolution at your previous confession, tell this to the Priest at once, and tell him the reason also why it was refused you. It is necessary also to mention that you did not go to Communion after your last confession, if that should have been your Easter Communion.

Listen attentively to the advice or questions of the confessor and do not interrupt him while he is speaking. If you have not understood the penance, ask him to repeat it after he has finished his admonition.

Unless the Priest has told you expressly to perform the penance every day, it is meant only for the one time.

Repeat the act of contrition whilst the Priest is pronouncing the prayers of absolution.

If you do not know the act of contrition by heart, ask the confessor to say it with you, as it is required to express one's contrition or sorrow in the sacrament of penance.

If absolution has been refused you, be sure to know the reason for it before you leave the confessional. Know exactly what the confessor demands of you before you can receive absolution and be admitted to Holy Communion, and when you are to return to him. Comply at once with his advice, and return to him at the time he had appointed.

Do not go to another confessor, when you know the one who refused you absolution, has requested or expects your return to him.

If you could not comply with the confessor's advice, or did not succeed in doing what he enjoined, return to him, nevertheless, at the time he had appointed, unless he should be absent.

Do not put off your confession indefinitely because absolution was refused you.

Many mistake the confessor's motive in denying them absolution, and imagine that it was because they had not been to confession for a long time. This is a great mistake. The confessor is always glad when sinners come to confession. There are always other reasons for putting off penitents to another time. The confessor must make sure of the sinner's disposition and firm purpose to do better, before he can, in many cases, accord him absolution. Inquire as to his motive, therefore, for refusing you absolution, be sure that you understand his instructions, return to him, and even if you should be put off again, try, try again. In view of the great evil of sin, and the eternity of its punishment, no number of attempts to do penance and become reconciled to God, ought to be too great.

Among the more common reasons for the refusal of absolution and for the prohibition to receive Holy Communion, are, for instance, habitual sinning; no improvement after repeated promises; living in the proximate occasion of sin, such as frequenting bad company, or saloons after repeated drunkenness; sinful company-keeping; unjust methods of business; secret societies; deadly enmity; neglect to make restitution after theft or injustice; neglect to repair calumny; the habitual missing of Holy Mass, and similar transgressions.

**How often "must" I go to Confession?** First: If I have had the misfortune to fall into a mortal sin, I must go to confession as soon after it as possible, and return as often as I had the misfortune to fall again. Secondly: I must go at least once in the year. This is the strict command of the Church.

**How often "should" I go to Confession?** As often as it is customary in my state of life. For children before their first Holy Communion, about every three months. For those who have received their first Holy Communion, and for young men and young women, every month where it is practical, or at least every three months. For parents and elderly persons settled in life, at least every three months.

## EXTREME UNCTION.

ALL persons dangerously ill, or in danger of death from sickness, wounds or accidents, are bound under pain of mortal sin to be anointed, or, in other words, to receive the holy sacrament of Extreme Unction.

### Sick=Calls.

### I. Calling the Priest.

**Never send a child to call the Priest.** Send a grown person. If there is no grown person in the house able to go, ask a neighbor to do so.

The sacraments of the dying are all too important and of too great a dignity, as that the arrangements for their administration should be made through children.

The Blessed Sacrament must not be carried through the streets unnecessarily, as often happens through calls being made by children, from whom the Priest cannot obtain exact information. Neither must the Priest be called out unnecessarily, as so often happens, likewise, through the calls of children who know not what to answer to the inquiries of the Priest.

Catholic neighbors must always be willing to assist one another on occasions of sickness and death.

Do not simply send for the Priest, but let the person who calls, be instructed as to what information he is to give to him.

The messenger should be able to give the following items:

1. Full name of the sick person; the correct address, that is, the name of the road or street, and the exact house-number.

These items are all the more important, if the Priest should not be at home and the call would have to be left in writing.

2. The age or condition of the person, whether child or grown person; whether practical Catholic.

3. Has the sick person been attended to before in the same sickness and by which Priest?

4. Which sacraments have been received and when?

5. Is the person able to receive Holy Communion, that is, is the sick person conscious or not subject to vomiting?

6. Has a physician attended and what is his opinion of the danger?

Whenever there is real danger, notify the Priest at once. Do not wait. Do not wait until evening or night.

Never call at night, on Saturday afternoon or evening, or on Sunday, except in case of sudden sickness, or when danger in delaying is apparent.

Do not call at the above-mentioned times for a sick person who has already been entirely attended to, unless the Priest has left word to that effect, or has not been to see the person for some time; or in case the sick person insists on it of his own accord, evidently from some trouble of mind.

If a sick call is made at night, let a gentleman accompany the Priest to and fro, until the Priest dispenses with his company.

**Let no one speak to the Priest** on the way, whilst he carries the Blessed Sacrament, except what is strictly necessary, or until he himself begins to speak.

It is not necessary to call the Priest for sick infants, as long as they have been baptized; but it is necessary in the case of children of seven years or even of younger children, if they have attained the use of reason. It may be necessary to give the latter absolution at least, if not to anoint them.

## II. Preparation of the Sick Person.

THE sick person must be forewarned of the Priest's coming, and must be advised to prepare for confession and the possible reception of the last sacraments.

Only when there is no immediate danger of death, and the Priest is called merely to speak to a sick person under peculiar circumstances, may the latter be left ignorant of the Priest's intended visit. But the Priest must consent to this arrangement, and not, by being left in ignorance of it, be brought into any embarrassing situation.

Attend to the sick person's appearance. See that it is clean and neat. Have face, hands and feet washed and the hair put in order.

When Holy Communion is to be administered, see that some preparation by prayer be made. If the sick person is unable to read, it is good for some one to read a few short prayers slowly and devoutly from a prayer-book, if circumstances will permit.

If there is danger of death and the Priest is to administer the last sacraments, or Holy Communion as Viaticum, the sick person need not be fasting, but may take whatever food, drink, or medicine may be necessary.

### III. Preparation of the Sick-Room.

HAVE the sick-room in good order by the time the Priest arrives, perfectly clean and tidy. Have all unsightly objects removed, such as soiled linens, dishes and vessels used by the sick person. Let the articles that must remain, be perfectly clean and presentable.

Have clean linens and coverings put on the bed.

Have no dog, cat or other animal in the room or in the parts leading to it.

Have a small table with a clean white cover opposite the sick-bed or at some distance from it, so that it can be seen by the sick person.

# SICK-CALLS. 85

A GOOD ARRANGEMENT.

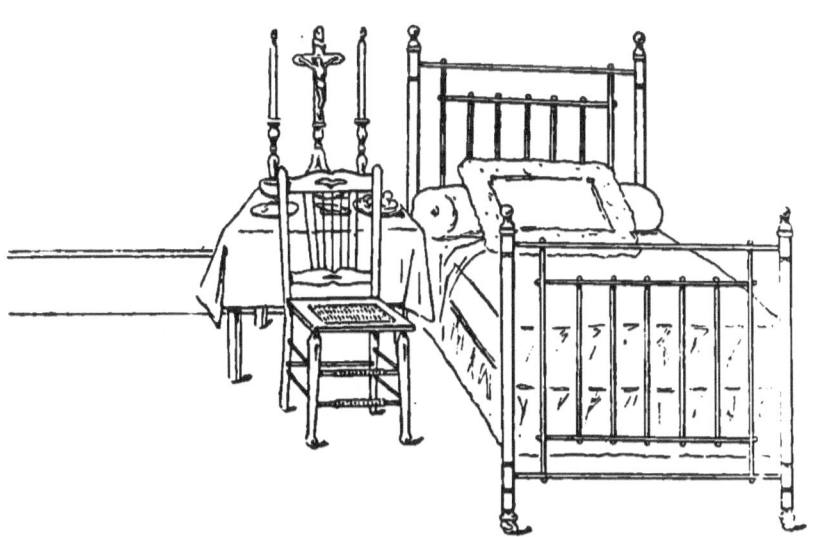

A BAD ARRANGEMENT.

## ARRANGEMENT OF THE SICK-ROOM.

Do not place it right next to the bed at the head of it, if it can be avoided.

Have a chair immediately next to the bed at the sick person's head for the Priest, so that he may look toward the foot of the bed and not into the sick person's face when he hears the confession.

### IV. Articles for the Sick=Room.

1. **A small table** or stand, at least two feet at the top, with a clean white cover.
2. **One crucifix** standing on the table or hanging directly over it for handing to the sick person to be kissed. Do not have the holy water-font attached to it.
3. **Two pure wax candles,** or one at least, in suitable candlesticks.
4. **One small vase** or glass of holy water (not Easter water) with a small sprig or brush for sprinkling.
5. **One small glass** of fresh drinking-water and **spoon.**
6. **One clean white cloth,** napkin or small towel, as a Communion cloth.

1. Table with white cover.
2. Crucifix.
3. Pure Wax Candle.
4. Vase of Holy Water.
5. Glass of Water and Spoon.
6. White Napkin.

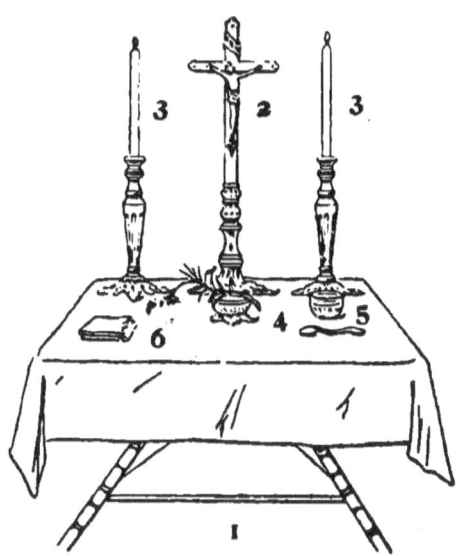

ARRANGED FOR COMMUNION.

7. Plate with Six Balls of Cotton.
8. Plate with Salt or Crumbs of Bread.
9. Finger=Bowl.

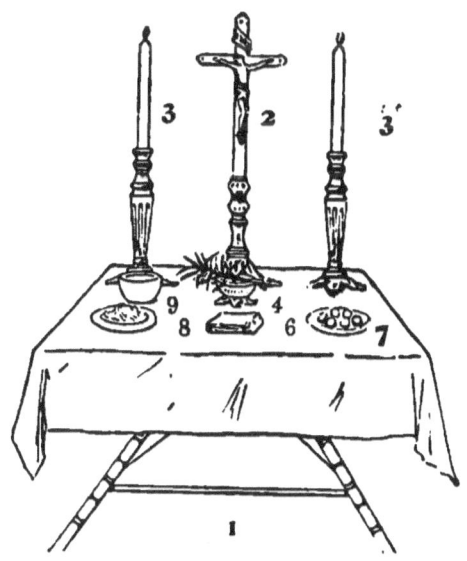

ARRANGED FOR EXTREME UNCTION.

## SICK-ROOM TABLE.

7. In the case of Extreme Unction being administered, also a small plate containing **six small balls of white cotton** of the size of large plums, and

8. **A small plate with salt** or small pieces of fresh bread without crust, for the cleansing of the Priest's fingers after anointing, together with a finger-bowl with water and a towel.

Have nothing else but the above-mentioned articles on the sick-room table. Keep all medicine-bottles, spoons, glasses and other objects not needed for the administration of the sacraments on another table or stand.

## V. Administration of the Sacraments.

THE following rules suppose the bringing of Holy Communion to the sick person.

As soon as the Priest arrives at the house, let someone meet him at the door with a lighted candle, and having bent the knee before the Blessed Sacrament which he carries, lead him to the sick-room.

Let none bid him the time of the day or begin to speak to him, unless what is strictly necessary, and that in a low tone of voice.

Let all others drop on their knees as soon as they meet the Priest, in whatever place they may be, and then follow him to the sick-room.

All should remain kneeling in the sick-room or in the place adjoining it, as space will permit, whilst the Priest pronounces the blessing and sprinkles the room, and not retire until bidden by him, when he is about to hear the confession.

Do not run away when the Priest comes; but let all endeavor to be present when he administers the rites of religion. Arrange your dress and put on a respectable appearance. Let no one be present in his shirt-sleeves, or with bare arms and the like.

When the Priest has heard the confession of the sick person and gives the signal, all should re-enter the room and remain kneeling in devout prayer until the Priest has finished his administrations.

If at any time before the Priest administers Holy Communion, it is necessary to pass before the sick-room table, the knee must be bent before it as in passing before the altar in church.

If anyone is familiar with the Latin prayers, he should answer to them.

Somebody should be ready to assist the Priest, especially during the anointing, to see that the ears, hands and feet of the sick person are uncovered and properly presented for the unctions.

Whatever articles of devotion may be required for the sick-room, have the Priest bless them before he retires, such as an indulgenced crucifix for the sick person to hold, a pair of beads, the scapulars and the like.

## VI. After the Administration of the Sacraments.

HAVE a crucifix or picture of the crucifixion, an image of our Blessed Lady, or other devout images placed about the sick-room in view of the sick person, so that he may frequently raise his heart to God at the sight of them.

Sprinkle the sick person occasionally with holy water, especially in his last agony.

Listen attentively to the instructions the Priest may leave, especially as to calling him again. Call him only in accordance with these instructions.

The water, bread, salt, cotton or other matter with which the Priest has purified his fingers, must be thrown into the fire.

## VII. Assisting the Dying.

As it is not always possible for a Priest to be present at the actual moment of death, especially in large parishes, and more especially where the parish covers a large territory, the faithful should themselves endeavor to assist their dying brethren after the Priest has administered the last Sacraments.

When they see that the patient's end is approaching, they should light a blessed candle and assist him to hold it in his hand, at least during the regular prayers for the dying and in the actual moment of death. If the agony should last a considerable time, some one else may hold the candle near by and keep it in readiness.

Some one should read the prayers for the dying from the prayer-book as well as other prayers after them, if the death-agony should continue.

If the agony should last very long, those and other prayers may be repeated from time to time.

The person holding the candle or kneeling close to the dying person, should from time to time, and especially at the last moment, repeat short and fervent in vocations to him, such as: "My Jesus, mercy." "My Jesus, forgive me my sins; I am heartily sorry for them." "Sweet Heart of Mary, be my salvation." "Jesus, Mary and Joseph, assist me." "Jesus, Mary and Joseph, into your hands I commend my body and my soul." "Lord, not my will, but Thine be done." "Father, into Thy hands I commend my spirit." "Angel Guardian and my Holy Patron, assist me," etc., etc.

Sprinkle the dying person often with holy water, especially if he should seem to have a hard struggle.

Let not too many persons crowd into the death-chamber, especially if it is small. If there should be many visitors, let them remain but a short time to say some prayers and then retire.

Do not sit around in the sick-room or adjoining rooms, unless you are sure you will be needed and can be of assistance.

## FUNERALS.

As soon as a member of your household has died, have the Priest notified at once, so that he may arrange matters for the funeral and have prayers said for the deceased.

Select a good Catholic undertaker at once, so that he may also arrange the funeral services and confer with the Priest.

By engaging a Catholic undertaker, you will save both yourself and the Priest much annoyance, as a Catholic undertaker is familiar with the regulations of the Church and burying-ground, as well as with the Catholic funeral service.

Remember funerals are an almost daily affair with most Priests, and if they cannot depend upon the existing regulations and customs for conducting them, but must be consulted repeatedly in each case, they are very much annoyed and embarrassed.

Therefore, abide by the existing regulations and do not ask for exceptions in your own case, as though it were a matter or calamity of rare occurrence.

Only those are entitled to a Catholic funeral service and burial in consecrated ground, who die in full communion with the Church. Hence, unbaptized persons; infidels; apostates; heretics; suicides; those who die from the effects of a duel, even if repentant; excommunicated Catholics, such as members of secret societies specially condemned by the Church; and public notorious sinners, dying without reconciliation, are excluded from such Catholic burial. As for non-practical Catholics, who may die suddenly without a chance to receive the sacraments, recourse is usually had to the Bishop. If the latter should see fit to refuse Christian burial to such, his judgment becomes the just punishment of the Church. It is useless to cite similar cases against such decisions.

As soon as the sick person has rendered his soul to God, all parties should kneel and say appropriate prayers, especially those given in the prayer-book for the departed soul.

All Catholics who come to view the remains, should also kneel for a few minutes at least, and say a prayer.

Prayers should be said from time to time, especially by those who watch at the corpse.

In some places parties watch with the dead all night, in others only for a time and then all retire as usual for the night.

This latter practice, if at all expedient, is at least preferable to the old-fashioned **wake,** so much deplored by the authorities of the Church, as well as by most respectable people; which latter observance is frequently only an apology for a so-called good time, consisting in smoking, drinking, card-playing and boisterous conduct;

disrespectable to the dead, disedifying, if not scandalous in the eyes of all devout Christians.

Let gentlemen who are staying really through charity with the bereaved family, but cannot abstain from smoking, retire to another room from that of the death-chamber for that purpose.

Let the death-chamber be characterized by profound quiet, devout praying and the light of blessed candles.

Have a crucifix, holy water and other articles of Catholic devotion and custom suitably arranged in the death-chamber. It is appropriate also to place a small crucifix, pair of beads, or the like in the hands of the deceased.

Avoid useless expense for flowers, but rather have Masses said for the soul of the departed one.

Many devout Catholics send their condolence with an offering for a Mass enclosed in an envelope, instead of a perishable and expensive floral offering.

Remember flowers are prescribed for the coffins of innocent children, but are discountenanced by the Church for the coffins of adults during the funeral service. Regulations made to this effect by our Bishops, are abused by Catholics in many places.

In some places the floral offerings are removed from the coffin at the church-door and are replaced after the funeral service has been performed.

Remember the regular funeral service of the Church is the Funeral Mass followed by the absolution of the dead.

Funerals without a Mass, in the afternoon, or performed privately at home, should occur only through unavoidable circumstances, such as too many funerals at one time, impossibility to put off the funeral to the opportune time, or contagious disease. In these cases a Mass should be said either on the funeral day itself, or on the following or next available morning with as many of the chief mourners present as possible.

Let the funeral **be on time.** Late coming is annoying both to the Priest and to the undertaker. They both have their engagements. Late funerals rob the Priest of his time and destroy his order and discipline. They also injure the business and success of the undertaker, who is liable to be placed between two fires both to please the funeral parties and to accommodate the Priest.

If the Priest should begin the Mass on the stroke of the appointed hour, and the corpse be brought in after the Mass has begun, let none but late comers be blamed. Other services and engagements of the Priest, or an incorrigible habit on the part of the people, occasionally necessitate such a course.

If you foresee that the funeral cannot be on hand at the usual hour, make special arrangements beforehand; but when the hour has been fixed, adhere to it, the same as if the corpse had to be brought to the train. Church-services should not be delayed any more than trains.

Do not ask for special privileges or distinctions, such as for a sermon, where it is not customary; for special music or singing not in harmony with the service of the Church, or the regulations of the parish.

Do not insist on having a friend, possibly a non-Catholic, sing a non-Catholic, sentimental selection in contrast to the severe, chaste music and language of the Church.

Do not attempt to have the coffin opened in or about the church. This is against the rules. Opening it in the cemetery is also a much to-be-deplored practice. People entitled to view the remains of a private individual, should do so at the funeral residence.

Do not ask the Priest to go to the cemetery unless it is his rule to do so, or unless you are entitled to it by special parish-regulations existing in favor of certain designated individuals, such as church or society-officials, special benefactors, members of the choir, or sanctuary, or the like.

Have only a few carriages in favor of a limited number of near relatives and very intimate friends. If there is a special regulation in this matter, be sure to observe it.

Have a Mass sung, or said at least, on the seventh day after the funeral; likewise on the thirtieth day, called the Month's Mind, and on each recurring anniversary.

Have Masses said also at other times according to your means, and give alms in favor of the dead rather than spend much money on floral designs, showy tomb-stones and meaningless monuments. Many Catholics spend vast sums of money on mere blocks of granite and marble for useless curbing, coping and paving of cemetery-lots, only to make the cemetery resemble a vast stone-yard rather than a neat garden or park.

# MATRIMONY.

REMEMBER that marriage with Christians is a sacrament, and needs a careful preparation. Otherwise this sacrament may be received unworthily, and an unhappy life, as is so often the case, may be the consequence.

When marriage has been decided upon, make arrangements as soon as possible with the Pastor.

Do not fix the date and hour yourselves, but consult the Priest and fix the time with him.

Remember, the law of the Church requires marriage-parties to be called out in their parish-church on three consecutive Sundays or holydays. This law is binding under pain of grievous sin. These announcements are called the **Bans of Matrimony.**

If there is any reason for not being called out three times, or for not being published at all, the reason must be made known to the Bishop.

Such preliminaries of matrimony require time, in order to comply with the laws of the Church, or to obtain the necessary dispensations from them. Hence the necessity of making **application to the Pastor at least three weeks in advance** of an intended marriage.

If there should be any impediment to the intended marriage from which it may be possible to obtain a dispensation, this must also be made known to the Bishop, together with the reasons for desiring to enter such a marriage.

If the Bishop sees fit to grant a dispensation from the bans of matrimony or from an impediment, the fine or penalty imposed by the Church for the same, must be paid, and whatever conditions may be prescribed must be fulfilled.

Engagements made with those of another religion, or with those with whom the laws of God or of the Church forbid matrimony, are not valid before the Church, and consequently not only do not bind in conscience, but are even sinful.

If the marriage-parties belong to different parishes, their bans of matrimony should be published in each parish.

Anyone aware of an impediment between the parties to be married, is bound in conscience to report the same to the Pastor.

The impediments of matrimony are:—
I. **Such as make a marriage null and void. Blood relationship** up to the fourth degree or third cousinship. **Affinity,** or relationship by marriage to the fourth degree or third cousinship of the husband or wife. **Spiritual Relationship** between Godparents or Sponsors and

those for whom they stand at baptism or confirmation, and the parents of the same, as well as between baptized persons and those who baptize them. **Public Honesty**, forbidding marriage with a parent, child, brother or sister of one with whom a valid engagement to marry had existed. **The Crime of Homicide or Adultery** on the part of persons, one of whom is married, with a view to subsequent marriage. **Difference of Worship,** that is, marriage between a baptized and an unbaptized person. **Vows** on the part of sacred ministers and religious who have pronounced solemn vows **Clandestinity** in places where the Decree of the Council of Trent has been published, declaring marriage null and void unless contracted before the Pastor and two witnesses. This decree obtains in the following places in the United States : in the States and Territories of Alabama, Arizona, Arkansas, California, Colorado, in the southern part of Indiana, Indian Territory, Louisiana,

Mississippi, Nevada, New Mexico, Texas, Utah, west of the Colorado River; the city of St. Louis, Missouri; the parishes of St. Genevieve, St. Ferdinand and St. Charles, belonging to the Archdiocese of St. Louis; the parishes of Kaskaskia, Cahokia, French Village and Prairie de Rocher, belonging to the Diocese of Alton, Illinois. **The Bond of previous marriage,** if both parties are still living. **II. Impediments which make a marriage unlawful,** but not null and void. Such are, **A Simple Vow** to observe chastity, to enter the priesthood or the religious state. **A Previous Valid Engagement** to marry someone. **The Forbidden or Closed Time** of Advent or Lent, that is, from the first Sunday of Advent until the seventh day of January, and from Ash Wednesday until the second Monday after Easter Sunday. **A Mixed Marriage,** that is, a marriage with a Christian or baptized person, but who is not a Catholic. **The Non-Consent of**

**Parents** when their consent is justly withheld.

If the marriage-parties belong to different parishes, they may choose either one of them, as a rule, for the marriage-ceremony. The church of the bride, however, is more usually the one in which the marriage is performed.

After arranging with the Pastor the time for the marriage-ceremony, a time should be appointed also for the marriage-instruction.

The marriage-instruction is all important, that the parties may be advised of the sacred and indissoluble character of matrimony, of the duties of husband and wife towards each other, as well as towards their children, and of the ceremonies that are to be performed in the reception of the sacrament.

It is customary for Catholics before entering the important state of matrimony, to make a **general confession** of their sins some weeks prior to the event.

Whether this confession is to be made of one's whole life, or only of a portion of it, will depend upon the decision of the confessor whose advice should be previously asked.

The bridal parties should confess also immediately before marriage, at least the evening before it.

Any doubts as to the obligations of the matrimonial state should be settled in the confessional.

Catholics should bear in mind that the marriage-ceremony is the principal thing about their wedding. All other observances are secondary. Marriage is a sacrament. Hence it would be a shame to curtail the religious part of it, or to avoid the expense or publicity of the same in preference to other bridal observances more popular with people of fashion; such as the bridal outfit, the breakfast, the wedding-tour or the future style of living.

The proper marriage-observance in the Catholic Church is the **Bridal** or **Nuptial**

**Mass.** It may be a High Mass or Low Mass, according to local custom or circumstances. Marriage without a Mass and especially in the evening, is not according to the spirit and intention of the Church, and is against the express wish of the Bishops of this country. The following are their words in the Third Plenary Council of Baltimore:

Let those who have the care of souls, take every occasion earnestly to exhort the faithful to the keeping of that pious and praiseworthy custom of the Church, whereby marriages are celebrated, not in the night-time, but during Mass, and accompanied by the **Nuptial Blessing.** * * * * This custom is held to be not merely a commendable but quite a necessary one, now in these present days, when the foes of religion are leaving nothing untried in their efforts to deprive, if possible, Holy Matrimony of all sanctity, and of all likeness to a sacrament, and to degrade it to the level of a mere civil contract. (Decrees, N. 125.)

Let them enter into marriage only through worthy and holy motives, with the blessings of religion, especially with the blessing of the Nuptial Mass. (Pastoral Letter, p. 87.)

The Nuptial Blessing can be given only at Mass. It can likewise, be given only once in a lifetime, so important is it; so that if a widow should marry again, she could not receive it, if it had been imparted to her at her first marriage.

A young woman, therefore, who is married in the evening or without a Mass, does not receive this bridal or nuptial blessing. What a shame to deprive oneself of such a blessing, so necessary for future happiness in the married state!

## The Marriage-Ceremony.

**Be on time.** Let this be the first observance. The Priest may have other engagements. In places where there is more than one Priest, the celebrant may begin the Mass on time, and arrange with another Priest to marry the bridal couple quietly at the altar-rail during the Mass.

A necessary treatment sometimes for late comers. Sometimes it is impossible for the celebrant to wait on account of other masses or services to follow.

Be in church before the Mass to make a preparation by prayer.

Kneel in the front pew or on special kneelers prepared for you, accordingly as it may be the custom. ,

Remove your gloves before you approach the altar. The marriage takes place immediately before the Mass.

If you go into the sanctuary according to custom, let the Groom walk first with the Bride at his left. Then follows the Groomsman or Best Man, with the Bridesmaid likewise at his left.

Make no genuflection until you reach the steps leading to the altar.

Let the Groomsman then go to the right of the Groom and the Bridesmaid to the left of the Bride and let all four then bend the knee together on the floor of the sanctuary and ascend together to the platform of the altar.

The Groom and Bride kneel on the edge of the platform, not on the upper step, but on the same level with the Priest. The Groomsman and Bridesmaid, however, stand respectively to the right and left of the bridal couple on the upper step or next lower level to the platform.

The following are the questions and answers which occur during the ceremony, with which the bridal couple should make themselves familiar:

PRIEST: (To the Groom.) N. Wilt thou take N. here present for thy lawful wife, according to the rite of our Holy Mother the Church?
GROOM: I will.
PRIEST: (To the Bride.) Wilt thou take N. here present for thy lawful husband according to the rite of our Holy Mother the Church?
BRIDE: I will.

The Bridegroom and Bride then join their right hands, and whilst so doing usually recite the following formula after the Priest, first the Bridegroom and then the Bride.

# MATRIMONY.

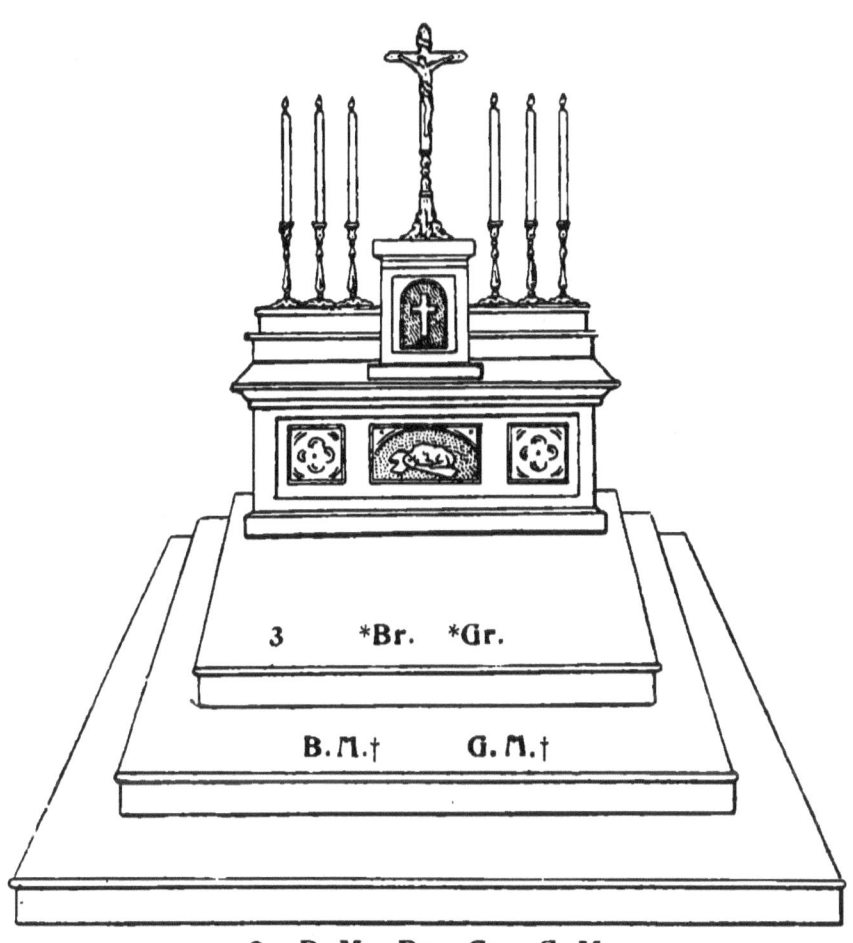

1. Going to the Altar. 2. Genuflecting before the lowest step. 3. Position during the marriage ceremony. * Kneeling. † Standing. Gr., Groom; Br., Bride; G. M., Groomsman; B. M., Bridesmaid.

## THE MARRIAGE CEREMONY.

BRIDEGROOM: I, N. N., take thee N. N. for my lawful wife, to have and to hold from this day forward, for better, for worse, for richer, for poorer, in sickness and in health, till death do us part.

BRIDE: I, N. N., take thee N. N. for my lawful husband, to have and to hold from this day forward, for better, for worse, for richer, for poorer, in sickness and in health, till death do us part.

After these words the right hands are still kept joined until the Priest has made the sign of the cross over the bridal couple and has sprinkled them with holy water.

The Bridegroom then produces the ring and places it on the plate for the Priest to bless it.

When the Priest presents the ring to the Bridegroom after the blessing, the latter puts it on the third finger of the Bride's left hand, saying the following words, if the Priest suggests them:

With this ring I thee wed and plight unto thee my troth.

After a few more prayers by the Priest,

the bridal couple rise and with the Groomsman and Bridesmaid go down the steps, turning around completely, make a genuflexion towards the altar on the floor of the sanctuary, and return, the Groom and Bride walking first, to their places.

During the Pater Noster of the Mass, the **Groom and Bride only** go up to the platform of the altar again, in the same manner as before the Mass, and again kneel immediately behind the Priest on the edge of the platform.

They remain kneeling there whilst the Priest says the prayers over the Bride, and return to their seats again, when he turns to the altar and continues the Mass.

It is customary for the Groom and Bride at least, to receive Holy Communion.

During the last prayers of the Mass, at the epistle side, the **Groom and Bride only** go up to the altar again and kneel as on the previous occasions, immediately behind the Priest on the platform of the altar.

They remain there attentive to his prayer and to the exhortation he may think proper to give, and do not retire until he has sprinkled them with holy water and has imparted both to them and to the congregation the blessing of the Mass.

They remain in prayer and in thanksgiving at their places some minutes after the Mass, whilst the Priest makes his thanksgiving, and whilst the congregation leaves the church. They should not leave the church immediately after the Mass, especially if they have received Holy Communion.

They should then have their marriage recorded in the parish-register. To have it done before the marriage, so as to expedite matters after the marriage-ceremony, is not the correct thing. It is not a truthful record and is often attended with mistakes and difficulties.

If a license is required by the State, the certificate must be shown to the Priest before the ceremony and signed by him after it.

The marriage-fee, as well as the offering for the Mass, should be paid before the ceremony takes place.

Do not ask for special privileges in your case or for exceptions to the general regulations of the parish or of the Church. This embarrasses the pastor very much. One exception thus made may justify twenty others, and thus the Pastor is hampered in his efforts to have order and to do justice to all his parishioners. If you are prominent in the parish by the active interest you take in its affairs, you may rest assured that you will be honored in more than one way without asking the distinction yourself.

If your prominence in the parish is due only to your wealth or to your popularity outside of the Church, it is not fair to make the Church sacrifice her rules and regulations to privilege you above others, who are perhaps more deserving members of the Church, even though they are poor and unpretending.

Do not mix up worldly, protestant or even heathen observances with the matrimonial customs and ceremonies of your Church. Let no rice be thrown in or near the sacred edifice of the True Temple of God. There is no marriage-ceremony more appropriate, beautiful and edifying, than that of the Catholic Church, when fully carried out according to her rules and privileges. But when her ceremonial is rejected, foolish, un-Catholic practices will be substituted.

Do not ask that the Church be specially decorated for the occasion, or go to expense for the purpose, unless you have been accustomed to decorate or embellish the church on other more sacred occasions. Such conduct is pure vanity and self-adoration.

A bridal tour is preferable to a wedding-banquet carried into all hours of the night, and even into the next morning, with drinking, dancing and boisterous behavior to the disedification and annoyance of all respectable people.

## THE PRECEPTS OF THE CHURCH.

THE observance of the Precepts or Commandments of the Church is binding upon every Catholic under pain of grievous sin or of eternal damnation. "If he will not hear the Church," says our Blessed Saviour, "let him be to thee as the heathen and publican." Matth. 18, 17

## THE OBLIGATION TO HEAR MASS.

EVERY Catholic who has attained the use of reason, is bound under pain of mortal sin to hear Mass on Sundays and holydays of obligation.

**The Holydays of Obligation or of Precept** in the United States are :—

1. **January 1st, Feast of the Circumcision of our Lord.**
2. **Feast of the Ascension of our Lord,** on Thursday, the fortieth day after Easter Sunday.
3. **Feast of the Assumption of the Blessed Virgin Mary, August 15th.**
4. **Feast of All Saints, November 1st.**
5. **Feast of the Immaculate Conception of the Blessed Virgin Mary, December 8th.**
6. **Feast of the Nativity of our Lord, or Christmas, December 25th.**

The above-named feasts and no others are holydays of obligation, on which days one is obliged to hear Mass under pain of mortal sin, unless some grave and unavoidable reason should prevent it.

**Just reasons for missing Mass** on Sundays and holydays of obligation may be, for instance: Sickness, such as confines the patient to the house, or such as is not so serious, but which exposure to the weather would probably aggravate so as to render it dangerous. The necessity for someone to remain at home, to watch the house, wait on the sick, prepare the food and the like. Minding children on the part of mothers and nurses when they have no one to take their place. The husband is ordinarily obliged to mind the baby whilst the wife hears Mass, unless the child is sick or unusually cross. Great distance, that is, several miles from the church for those who are obliged to walk when the roads are bad. A great distance, likewise, for those who have to ride, when the weather and the roads are very bad, even for vehicles. Not sufficient riding-accommodation, so that some are obliged to remain at home when the others go to church; in which case, however, the members of the family are obliged to go in turns. Inability to leave off one's occupation, with danger of losing one's position. Great repugnance arising from modesty if one be exposed to public notice and comment under unavoidable circumstances. The lack of sufficient and decent clothing in time of great poverty.

If anyone may have missed Mass through these or other reasons, it is well to mention the fact in confession, even though the reason may have been legitimate, so that the confessor may give his approval or disapproval of the act, accordingly as the penitent may have acted conscientiously or unscrupulously.

Catholics easily get into the habit of missing Mass for insufficient and trifling reasons.

Being a stranger in a place and not knowing where the church is, is not of itself a sufficient reason for missing Mass. We are obliged to make inquiries and efforts to find a Catholic church when in a strange place.

Neither is it a sufficient reason to miss Mass if the church at hand should be for the use of another nationality, the language of which we do not understand. The Mass itself is in the Latin tongue; attendance at it is binding upon all nationalities alike under pain of mortal sin.

Those who are prevented from attending Mass on a Sunday or holyday of obligation, through any legitimate cause, do well to say the Mass-prayers at home at the time of the Mass, if convenient, or perform some other devotion instead.

**Don't come late to Mass!** It is a sin not only to miss Mass altogether, but also to come late to it through one's own fault.

It is a grievous sin, however, to miss the principal parts of the Mass by coming late through one's own fault.

The principal parts of the Mass are: the Offertory, the Consecration or Elevation, and the Communion.

Whoever, therefore, has missed the Offertory by coming late through his own fault, and does not hear another Mass, is guilty of a grievous sin.

Hearing Mass according to the precept of the Church, means not only coming to Mass and being present at it during its course; it means also actually attending to it by following the action of the Priest, and performing some devotion at the same time.

**Don't remain in the rear of the Church!** Those who purposely and by habit remain in the rear of the church in a great crowd of people and are consequently constantly distracted and unable to see, hear or follow the Priest properly at the principal parts of the Mass, and who at the same time perform no particular devotion, do not hear Mass according to the command and intentions of the Church, and are guilty of sin, which they are bound to confess, as though they had not gone to Mass at all.

**Don't come to Mass without a prayer-book!** especially if you are in the habit of hearing Mass on Sundays and holydays only.

Devout Catholics hear Mass also on other days besides Sundays and holydays. But such days are not of precept, but of devotion, and it is not a sin to miss Mass on them. Such days are: The Feast of the Epiphany, January 6th; Candlemas Day, February 2; Ash Wednesday; St. Patrick's Day, March 17; Feast of St. Joseph, March 19; Feast of the Annunciation, March 25; Holy Thursday, Good Friday and Holy Saturday; Rogation Days, April 25, and the three days before Ascension Day; the Feast of Corpus Christi; the Feast of the Sacred Heart of Jesus; All Souls' Day, November 2; the first Friday of each month in honor of the Sacred Heart of Jesus; the days of Advent and Lent, and during the months of May and October. But no one commits a sin by not hearing Mass on these days, and it should not be made matter of confession

## FASTING AND ABSTAINING.

Do not confound the obligation of fasting with that of abstaining. They are two distinct things.

By fasting is meant, not eating, or eating only a certain quantity of food as fixed by the Church.

By abstaining is meant, keeping from certain kinds of food, especially from flesh-meat.

### I. Fasting.

THE Church commands all Catholics who have completed their twenty-first year, and have not attained a recognized old age, or who are not otherwise legitimately dispensed, to fast under pain of committing a grievous sin.

The mere fact that one had never fasted before, although he may be over twenty-one years of age and has the required health for so doing, does not excuse from the obligation to fast under pain of mortal sin.

Such as are obliged to fast, are allowed to take only one full meal on fast-days ordained by the Church.

At this full meal anything may be eaten, except meat, if it should happen to be on an abstinence day; (see Abstinence Days, page 132), or fish during Lent, if meat should be a part of the meal.

Meat and fish at the same meal are not permitted, even on Sundays during Lent.

If the full meal be taken at noon, then the breakfast dare not exceed the matter and quantity regulated by approved custom.

This breakfast consists only of a warm drink, such as coffee, tea or chocolate, slightly sweetened, and a slice or two of bread; say about two ounces, or equal quantity of biscuits, crackers, or the like. Such eatables as butter, eggs, cheese, fruit and the like are not permitted at this breakfast, and milk only in sufficient quantity to merely color the warm drink.

At the evening collation the fourth part of an ordinary meal is permitted. No meat is permitted at this repast, as it is the collation of one fasting.

If the full meal be taken in the evening, however, then meat will be permitted at it on a non-abstinence day. In this case then, the equivalent of the evening collation can be taken in the morning, and the breakfast as luncheon at noon, thus inverting the above-mentioned order.

## Who are not obliged to fast?

Those who have not completed their twenty first year.

Those of advanced age.

The sick and infirm, who cannot fast without positive injury to their health.

Hard-working people and such who feel that they cannot perform their work properly, when they fast, and that they thereby injure their health.

Women who are pregnant or who are nursing.

Those who by their occupation, are exposed to all kinds of weather, and to irregularity in getting their meals.

Persons having doubts about their obligation to fast or abstain, should consult their confessor or any Priest whom it is convenient for them to meet. It is advisable always to be governed in this matter by the decision of the Priest.

Those who cannot comply with the fast and abstinence as enjoined by the Church, ought to practice some other good work or mortification instead. It is well to abstain, for example, from intoxicating drinks.

**Fast-Days in the United States ordinarily are:**

1. All Fridays in Advent.
2. Every day in Lent except Sunday.

**3. All Wednesdays, Fridays and Saturdays in the Ember Weeks,** that is the Wednesday, Friday and Saturday following the first Sunday in Lent; the Wednesday, Friday and Saturday following Whitsunday or Pentecost; the Wednesday, Friday and Saturday following the 14th day of September, and the Wednesday, Friday and Saturday following the third Sunday of Advent.

**4. The following Vigils of feasts: Saturday before Whitsunday; August 14,** Vigil of the feast of the Assumption; **October 31,** Vigil of the feast of All Saints, and **December 24,** Vigil of Christmas.

## II. Abstinence.

THE Church prohibits the use of flesh-meat on certain days under pain of mortal sin, to all Catholics who have attained the use of reason.

Thus, in most countries, every Friday of the year is a day of abstinence from flesh-meat, except Christmas Day.

During Lent, even on Sundays, the Church prohibits also the use of fish and flesh-meat at the same meal; so that only one of the two kinds of food may be taken at the same time.

The Church counsels also abstaining from intoxicating liquors on certain days in consideration of her dispensations from the old and severe laws of fasting and abstinence.

The use of eggs, milk, butter and cheese is permitted on all fast and abstinence-days, except at the breakfast of those who are obliged to fast; who may use a slight quantity of milk, however, in the warm drink permitted in the morning. Besides lard, the fat rendered from any kind of meat may be used in preparing food on any day of fasting or abstinence throughout the year.

## Who are not obliged to abstain?

THE sick, whose condition is one of great weakness, so that strengthening food like meat, is absolutely necessary for them.

Those, who, through great poverty, through traveling, working or stopping away from home, have nothing or scarcely anything else at the time to eat.

Those who, living with non-Catholics, cannot be accommodated with anything else; especially after having made known their custom and desire to abstain from flesh-meat.

**Abstinence Days in the United States ordinarily are:**

1. **All Fridays of the year,** except Christmas Day.

2. **All Wednesdays in Lent.**\*

---

\*All days of Lent are days of abstinence by the general law of the Church. But by an indult of the Holy See, granted August 3, 1887, for ten years, the use of flesh-meat is allowed, once a day only, on Mondays, Tuesdays, Thursdays and Saturdays for those who are obliged to fast, the second and last Saturday of Lent excepted. As for those who are not obliged to fast, meat is

3. **All Wednesdays and Saturdays in Ember weeks,** that is: The Wednesday and Saturday following the first Sunday in Lent; the Wednesday and Saturday following Whitsunday or Pentecost; the Wednesday and Saturday following the 14th day of September, and the Wednesday and Saturday following the third Sunday of Advent.

4. **The following Vigils of feasts: Saturday before Whitsunday; August 14,** Vigil of the feast of the Assumption; **October 31,** Vigil of the feast of All Saints; **December 24,** Vigil of Christmas.

By an indult of the Holy See granted March 15, 1895, for ten years in favor of workingmen, the Bishops of this country may dispense the former from the more rigid law of abstinence in view of certain difficulties that may exist in their dioceses. In virtue of this indult, workingmen to-

permitted more than once on the above-mentioned days. Flesh-meat is permitted for everyone at all meals on Sundays.

gether with their entire households may eat flesh-meat on the abstinence days of Lent, on Ember days and on the Vigils of the feasts, except on Fridays, on Ash Wednesday, on the days of Holy Week and on the Vigil of Christmas. As flesh-meat, however, is permitted by the indult of August 3, 1887, on all Mondays, Tuesdays and Thursdays of Lent, Wednesday and Saturday are the only days remaining in Holy Week on which the use of flesh-meat is not permitted. Those who are obliged to fast, however, can avail themselves of this dispensation only at the principal meal.

In desiring to make use of this indult in favor of workingmen, the faithful must make sure, that it is in use in their respective diocese.

If on any day you are in doubt about the obligation to abstain or the privilege to eat meat, consult the following rules:—

**Rule 1. No meat at all for anyone:** All Fridays of the year, Ash Wednesday,

Wednesday in Holy Week, Holy Saturday and the day before Christmas.

**Rule 2. No meat at all for those who are obliged to abstain, but are not obliged to fast,** who are not workingmen, where they are specially dispensed, or are not of the latter's households.

All Fridays of the year, Ash Wednesday, all Wednesdays in Lent, Holy Saturday, all Ember days, the Vigils of the feasts of Pentecost, Assumption of the Blessed Virgin Mary, of All Saints and of Christmas.

**Rule 3. No meat at all for those who are obliged to fast:** All Fridays of the year, all Wednesdays in Lent, Holy Saturday, Wednesdays and Saturdays in the Ember Weeks, and the Vigils of the feasts of Pentecost, Assumption of the Blessed Virgin Mary, of All Saints and of Christmas.

**Rule 4. Meat once a day only for those who are obliged to fast:** All Mondays, Tuesdays, Thursdays and Satuı days in Lent, except the second Saturday in Lent, which is an Ember Day, and Holy Saturday. Also on all abstinence Wednesdays of the year, for those who live together with workingmen, where the latter are specially dispensed, except the days mentioned in **Rule 1**.

**Rule 5. Meat three times a day**: On all Sundays of Lent for everyone; on Mondays, Tuesdays, Thursdays and Saturdays of Lent for those who are not obliged to fast, except the second Saturday of Lent, which is an Ember Day, and Holy Saturday. On all days of the entire year and of Lent even, for workingmen and such of their households as are not obliged to fast, where the special dispensation has been given, except the days mentioned in **Rule 1**.

## ANNUAL CONFESSION.

ALL Catholics who have attained the use of reason, and are in sin, even if they have not yet received their first Holy Communion, or whether they are able to go to Holy Communion or not, are obliged to confess their sins to the Priest at least once during the year under pain of mortal sin.

Hence, small children who may be supposed to have the use of reason, must be prepared and sent to Confession.

This annual confession is not the Easter duty, although the time usually fixed for it, begins at Easter and extends to the following Easter.

The Easter duty concerns Holy Communion.

The confession, however, made in compliance with one's Easter duty, suffices also for the fulfilling of this duty of annual confession.

An adult who goes neither to confession nor to Communion during a whole year, is guilty, therefore, of breaking two distinct precepts of the Church.

This annual confession may be made to any Priest empowered in a place to hear confessions.

## THE EASTER DUTY.

THE Easter duty is the obligation of every Catholic of requisite age to receive Holy Communion within the Easter time.

This obligation begins at about the twelfth year and continues throughout life. During this time it binds under pain of mortal sin all those who enjoy the use of reason.

The Easter time in this country extends from the First Sunday of Lent until Trinity Sunday.

The precept binds all grown Catholics of sound mind without distinction, whether they are in health or in sickness, whether they are able to go to church or not.

Those who are not able to go to church during the Easter season, or those in charge of them, must notify the Priest, so that he may bring Communion to the former although they be in no danger of death.

Do not put off notifying the Priest until the last week, or second last week of the Easter time; but give him ample opportunity by notifying him in the beginning or in the middle of the Easter season; as he may have a great many invalids to attend to during the course of the Easter time.

To prepare a sick person properly for the performance of this duty, see article:

Communion for the Sick, page 65; and Article: Sick-Calls, page 79.

To make one's Easter duty, it is not necessary to receive on Easter Sunday, during Holy Week or during Easter Week. As for those who go to confession and Communion only once or twice in the year, they ought rather not to go to confession at a time when the confessor is busiest, as on Holy Saturday or Christmas Eve, as the Priest has all he can do to hear those who go frequently to Communion, and who are the more entitled to go on the great feast-days.

There is no such thing as a Christmas duty in this country. Hence it is not a sin if one does not go to the sacraments during the Christmas season; although it is advisable to do so, as the Church would have the faithful to go to Communion from time to time during the year.

It is not necessary in performing one's Easter duty to have the express intention of so doing. All that is necessary to fulfill one's duty, is to receive Holy Communion some time during the Easter season, whatever intention one may or may not have.

**Do not put off your Easter duty until the last week of the Easter time**, or even to the very last day of it. If the Priest at that time should not find it expedient to give you absolution, or admit you to Holy Communion, and the Easter time thus elapses before you receive, remember it will be your own fault, and you make yourself guilty of a grievous sin through your own carelessness.

## SUPPORT OF THE PASTOR AND OF THE CHURCH.

CATHOLICS are bound under pain of sin to contribute to the support of their Pastor and of his assistants.

In this country there is the obligation, likewise, to contribute to the building and maintenance of church and school.

Whatever means are adopted in the parish to this end, Catholics must be willing to do their share, whether it be by paying a fixed amount of dues, pew-rent, seat-money, or by contributing to certain collections and entertainments, and making certain customary offerings in receiving the administrations of religion.

## Who are obliged to contribute to this support?

ALL members of the parish who have an income of their own, whether they are married or single, whether they have families or not, whether they live with their families, board, or live for themselves. Moreover sons and daughters who pay their board, and have the balance of their income for their own use, are bound equally as well as their parents, to contribute to the support of Church, school and Pastor.

Those who have no children to send to church or school, must not think that they have less obligation to support the two institutions. Such a policy would be business, but not religion. On the contrary, the greater the means, the greater the obligation to support both church and school.

Servants and others having small salaries, must be willing to pay such dues as are fixed for them by their Pastor, as well as contribute to other sources of church-revenue.

Persons not able to pay the fixed dues, either through continued poverty, or for the time being, are bound to make their circumstances known to the Pastor, or be considered delinquents. To neither pay nor make any excuse to the Pastor, is considered either pure neglect of duty, or obstinacy.

Parties failing both to pay for their pews or seats, and to give an explanation for it, should remember that they forfeit their right to them. It requires no notice on the part of the Pastor to such, in order that he may be justified in disposing of their pew or seat in favor of others.

Whatever misunderstandings may exist between pew-holders and ushers, clerks and others, should be reported at once to those in charge, or to the Pastor himself.

Parties failing to report in due time, cannot expect their grievances to be adjusted afterwards to the discomfort of innocent parties.

Pay your dues or pew-rent at the appointed time and place, and see that you receive credit for it. Do not expect the Pastor or anyone else to carry the pew-book about with him. If through your neglect of these rules, and through your own awkwardness, you find that you have not been credited for your payment, you will have yourself to blame.

Parties unwilling to take part in church-entertainments or unable to attend them, should at least do their share by purchasing tickets or otherwise contributing to their object. If the character of such entertainments be not always to one's taste, the object of them, at least, should always be.

If you have been accidentally overlooked at a regular church-collection, either at one that is taken up within the church itself, or at a house-to-house collection in the parish, bring your contribution nevertheless, to the Pastor or to those in charge. Do not take advantage of such an oversight, when you would otherwise have contributed. Such conduct is too "small" for anyone calling himself a Catholic.

The duty of Catholics to support the Parochial school in particular, is put forth by the Bishops of this country among other urgent admonitions in the following appeal :

The laity should give a sufficient and generous support to the schools. They must, therefore, unite their efforts, so as to be able to meet all the necessary expenses for the Parochial school. The faithful must be reminded, be it in pastoral letters, be it in sermons or in private interviews, that they offend grievously against their duty if they neglect by every possible effort and expense to provide for Catholic schools.

This should be more especially brought home to the minds of those Catholics who are popular by their wealth and authority. Parents should, therefore, promptly and willingly pay the little monthly contribution which is exacted for each child.\* The other members of the parish, however, must not be unwilling to establish and increase any fund that may be necessary or reasonable for the maintenance of the schools. All, then, whether parents or other heads of families, or young people who have means of their own, should be ready to give their name to any institution, by which they may help by regular contributions, however small they may be, to support the schools, or to make them, if only in part, at least, free schools. The existence of such an institution in every parish is greatly to be recommended. Many of such have been established, and have been signally blessed by the Sovereign Pontiff. If all the faithful do

---

\*This sentence has reference to pay-schools.

their share towards this most sacred object, the result will be, improvement in the internal excellence as well as the external appearance of the school, increase of teachers on the one hand, and fewer children in the multiplied classes on the other, and consequently better grading throughout; all of which will wonderfully tend to raise the standard of our schools. (Acts and Decrees of the Third Plenary Council of Baltimore, No. 202).

## THE CLOSED TIME OF MARRIAGE.

THE Church forbids the faithful to solemnize a marriage during two particular seasons of the year, that is, from the first Sunday of Advent until the day after the feast of the Epiphany, January 7, and from Ash Wednesday until the Monday after Low Sunday, or the second Monday after Easter Sunday.

The Church does not prohibit marriage during this time, but only the usual ceremonies attending it, such as a nuptial or bridal Mass.

Only such marriages, however, should be performed during the closed time, as will suffer no delay through peculiar circumstances. They are celebrated privately, without pomp or splendor, before the Priest and the necessary witnesses.

## RELIGIOUS INSTRUCTION OF CHILDREN.

Parents must instruct their children in their religion at home before they are of age to go to school, as well as during the time they attend school or Sunday school.

Before the children are able to go to school or church for instruction, their parents should teach them from infancy, the name of God, how to make the sign of the cross, and the principal prayers.

Whilst the children attend religious instruction at church or at school, the parents must assist them in learning their catechism or make sure that they do learn it, and that they give satisfaction to their instructors. They dare not leave the task wholly to others, not even to the Priest himself, without any concern on their own part.

Parents are the first instructors of their children by the law of God, and have the first responsibility.

If the children should not have the advantage of a parochial or Sunday school, as in remote country places, the parents must assume the task of instruction themselves, as well as they are able, providing themselves with catechisms and other books of instruction; or intrust the task to others better qualified than themselves, but with their own supervision. They must occasionally, however, present the children to the Priest to be examined and to be prepared to receive the sacraments.

Parents should bring their children with them to church. They should not let them go there, as a rule, unattended, especially if they are very small, as they are liable to disbehave themselves there, not yet realizing the sacredness of the place.

Parents must not be content simply to leave their children in charge of their teachers, whether secular or religious. This will do, for example, at the regular children's Mass and at Sunday school, when it is impossible and undesirable for the parents to attend. But parents must make it a point to bring their children to church with them at other times.

Teachers may watch over the children in their charge to see that they keep quiet; but as these teachers usually have a large number of children under their care they cannot well attend to their individual conduct and devotion. This the parents must attend to themselves by bringing their children with them when they come to church; showing them how to conduct themselves in the house of God, how to act at the different parts of the Mass and at other services; correcting them each time that they show the slightest irreverence or want of devotion. Children left to themselves in church or even to the watching of a class-teacher only, rarely learn how to conduct themselves properly in church.

See that your children enter church quietly and respectfully; that they take holy water devoutly on entering; that they do not slam the door. See that they make the genuflection properly. See that they walk up the aisle slowly and reverently, not swinging their arms, or in the case of boys, not chewing their hats. See that they kneel and say a prayer before they sit down. See that they kneel, stand and sit properly, bow and strike their breasts devoutly at the proper times. Show them how to use the prayer-book and the beads, and see that they observe what is going on and explain to them the meaning of the various functions after the services are over.

Persons with a few children, or with only one to instruct in this manner, have all they can do besides attending to their own devotions. One in charge of a great number of children cannot perform these duties satisfactorily.

Thus must parents assist, introduce and supplement the work of training and instructing their children, otherwise carried on by the teachers.

Where there is a regular children's Mass, parents must not permit their children to go to any other, unless accompanied by themselves or other responsible adults and with the approval of the Pastor. In any other case, they must send them to the teachers or to the Pastor for special orders. They must not permit them to go to any Mass of their own accord contrary to Parish regulations.

## THE PAROCHIAL SCHOOL.

CATHOLIC parents and Catholics in general must do all in their power to aid their Pastors in the building and maintenance of Catholic or Parochial Schools.

The following quotation contains the burning words of the assembled Bishops of this country at the Third Plenary Council of Baltimore on this matter:—

"In regard to the laity (lay faithful) we exhort and command that they be so instructed by the Bishop and the Priests, that they learn to regard the Parochial school as an essential part of the parish, without which the future existence of the parish will be endangered. They are, therefore, to be made to understand clearly and thoroughly that the school is not, by any means, a mere devotional institution of the Priest's own free adoption for the purpose of manifesting his great zeal, or of spending his time pleasantly and usefully; but that it is a burden and a duty imposed upon the Priest by the Church, to be religiously executed by him, but not without the assistance and help of the laity. Not less zeal and wisdom should be employed to destroy that false notion in the minds of many of the faithful, that the Parochial school exists only for those members of the parish who use it for their own children, but it should be shown to them by plain argument that the benefits and blessings resulting from faith and morality preserved in the Parochial school, redound to the good of the whole community. The result of all this will be that the laity belonging to the parish will regard no other institution, after the parish church itself, more sacred, nor regard it with more solicitude than the Parochial school, as destined to preserve the faith and morals of their children, and to make them the prop and promise of society. (Acts and Decrees of the Third Plenary Council of Baltimore, No. 202.)

As for those who through peculiar circumstances cannot send their children to the parish-school, they are, nevertheless, bound to give their support to it.

See support of the Pastor and Church, page 141, and appended Decree of the Third Plenary Council of Baltimore, page 145.

In sending their children to school for

the first time, parents should invariably accompany them, that they may superintend their admission and make the acquaintance of the superintendent or principal, and of the respective teacher.

Parents must not attempt to send children to school who are too young, merely to get rid of them at home, where they feel them to be a burden.

Parents and guardians must not easily listen to every little complaint made by the children against the teachers, against other children, or against the school itself.

If they have a real grievance or are not satisfied with a child's conduct or progress, let them not at once run to the Pastor, but let them go first to the respective teacher, or to the principal, and endeavor to adjust the matter with them.

Let them have recourse to the Pastor only after they have failed to get satisfaction from the teachers themselves.

Let no one take a child out of school, least of all upon a complaint or grievance, without any further notice to those in charge.

No one ought to call upon a teacher, however, during school-hours to the interruption of the class. This is an injustice to the parents of the other children, as well as an injury to the school. Call upon the teacher immediately before or after school-hours, or at his residence.

Only then should parents visit the class-room during school-hours, when it is necessary to meet teacher and scholar together, or other children at the same time.

Parents must send their children to school on time, at the very beginning of the session, and especially after the summer vacation. The teacher must not be made to delay the progress of other children by helping on those who have come late and are, therefore, not as far advanced as the body of the class.

Parents must not be unreasonable in demanding the promotion or graduation of children who are not entitled to it, either through dulness, want of application or irregular attendance.

As for the last two causes, let the record of attendance and of the merits of the child be consulted. As for dulness, a child that cannot read and write correctly the lessons of the respective class, and is not able to do the ordinary sums that successful children in the same grade do, must not be expected to be promoted.

Children must not be kept out of school except through sickness and like unavoidable causes. Still less must they be taken out of school before the annual session or complete course is finished.

After each single time or term of absence parents should give their children a written excuse to present to the teacher; or what would be still better, send notice at once to the teacher when a child is kept at home. If this were observed invariably, the practice of truancy would become impossible.

Catholic schools, as a ru'e, cannot afford to employ truant-officers and other officials, as the State schools. The conscientiousness of Catholic parents, ought to make such officials altogether unnecessary.

Catholics should remember that lack of funds puts Catholic schools generally at a certain disadvantage compared to public schools; but by dint of patience, self-sacrifice and Christian forbearance on the part of Catholics, their schools can be made equal, if not superior, to their public competitors.

Hence Catholics should be willing to suffer some inconveniences, even misunderstandings and privations for the sake of extending to their children a solid Catholic education.

Parents and guardians should be prompt in signing all reports sent to them for their children, and conscientious in observing all the regulations of the school. They should call upon the teacher occasionally to certify the genuineness of their signatures; but especially should they visit the teacher, if the report is not satisfactory.

Books and stationery should be provided cheerfully by the parents, where the school is not able to supply these articles free of charge. When the books and school-goods, however, are furnished gratuitously, it is the bounden duty of both parents and children to take the most scrupulous care of them and to make good whatever damage or loss they have caused through their own carelessness.

Catholics should always bear in mind that Catholic teachers receive a trifling salary for their services, compared with public school teachers, thus saving the State and the people an enormous out'ay of money. They should not forget that they themselves would be taxed much higher for public education, if it were not for the self-sacrificing spirit of so many Catholic teachers, educating so many Catholic children, who would otherwise have to be taught by the State at a much larger expense.

## THE SUNDAY SCHOOL.

WHEREVER there is a Sunday school attached to a parish, whether it be for all the children of the parish, or only for such as do not attend the parochial school, the respective parents are obliged to send their children to it.

The children are bound to attend it up to such an age or such a degree of proficiency, as is fixed by the Pastor.

Parents or guardians should invariably accompany their children when they desire them to be admitted to Sunday school, that the Priest or superintendent may make the acquaintance of both the children and their parents.

Children that have received their first Holy Communion or have been confirmed, must, as a rule, still attend Sunday school until they have learned a larger catechism and the Bible-History, or have completed such an age as is fixed by the Pastor for their dismissal.

Parents should be acquainted with the teachers of their children. They should visit them occasionally, and make inquiries about their children. They should call upon them, especially when there is any trouble in regard to a child.

The parents must see to it that the children study the catechism during the week, spending some time at it every day along with their other lessons. Do not permit the children to put off their catechism-lesson until the end of the week or even until Sunday morning.

Parents must, moreover, sign the reports that are sent to them from the Sunday school; send a written excuse to the teachers when their children have been absent through any cause, or go in person to explain.

As the Sunday school has but little time accorded to it to accomplish the difficult task of instructing children in such an important and arduous branch of learning as the knowledge and practice of religion, the parents must be extremely particular in sending their children punctually and not allow them easily to miss a single instruction.

Let parents be grateful to the ladies and gentlemen who voluntarily assume the burden of instructing their children. Let them remember that these persons are volunteer teachers without compensation, taken from every avocation of life, often ill-suited to the task they are to perform, but doing, as a rule, the best they can; that they are often tired and worn out on Sunday, after a week's hard work, and are frequently sacrificing their week's rest and recreation in the cause of Christian doctrine.

Parents who have the choice of sending their children to a parochial school, where they are instructed in their religion daily by professional teachers of Christian Doctrine, should be the more easily satisfied with the pains that volunteer teachers take with the children once a week, and should be the more willing to overlook defects, which must necessarily exist under such meagre auspices of imparting Christian instruction.

The average Parish-Priest is very much occupied on Sunday. He cannot easily manage a large concourse of children in as short a space of time, as is usually allotted to Sunday school work, and at the same time do full justice to their religious instruction and training, attend to all their many calls upon him, as well as to those of their teachers and parents.

The average Sunday school must always remain at best a mere substitute and an apology for a parochial school.

Under these conditions, parents must not easily find fault with the Pastor and his staff of Sunday school teachers, but must rather strive to assist them by their own conscientiousness in observing the rules of the Sunday school, in sending their children punctually to its sessions and services, and in aiding the Pastor and teachers by also instructing the children themselves, or at least by supervising their catechism-lessons at home.

## RELIGION AT HOME.

The Church is not the only place for the practice of religion. The home is also a sacred place in which God must be especially honored and where the faith of Christians must be planted and fostered. "Your home is your Church." (*St. Augustine.*)

If religion is not taught and practiced at home, the church and school will scarcely be able to preserve it.

Let your home be Catholic by the presence of the crucifix and of other sacred images.

Have holy water in constant use.

Have the Bible in the principal room in an honored position, and have nothing else lying or placed on top of it. Have other Catholic books of edification and instruction, and have some Catholic papers and periodicals.

Keep out of your house trashy novels and sensational newspapers.

Do not permit your children, as a rule, to read novels and story-books which they borrow from other children, without your knowing anything about the character of such works. Let them read only such books as they obtain under Catholic auspices, as from a Catholic library or from experienced and strict Catholic people.

Keep out of your house pictures and representations of love-scenes and nudities, whether they be works of art, ornaments or mere advertisements.

Have all the religious articles necessary for sick-calls.

See Sick-Calls, Articles for the Sick-Room, page 86; and Blessings and Blessed Articles, page 168.

See that all the members of the household, especially the children, say their morning and night prayers. Attend to the children's prayers personally. Do not merely ask them whether they say their prayers, but go and see for yourselves. If children attempt to come to the breakfast-table without having said their morning prayers, make them return to their rooms. Say the prayers frequently with them, especially the night prayers.

Always insist on all members of the family saying grace before and after meals, and on reciting the Angelus at the sound of the church-bell.

Have special devotions in common in the evening, especially during Lent, Advent, during the month of October, on Ember days, and at other times. Say the rosary, the litanies and other prayers according to time and circumstances.

Read from the Bible, especially from the Gospels and Epistles, or from the small Bible-History. Let only those passages be read to the family with which the parents are familiar. Read also from the Catechism, the Lives of the Saints, and from other books of instruction and edification.

Read these rules of "*Catholic Practice*" at stated times, so that all may become familiar with the practice of their holy religion.

Make sure that the children learn their Catechism, by hearing their lessons either before they retire at night, or before they go to school to recite them.

Accustom the children to works of charity and mercy by supplying them with alms and means for the relief of poor and suffering neighbors. Make them do chores for poor and aged neighbors.

Try every day, if possible, to have one

member at least of the household attend Holy Mass, so that the family may always be represented at the Holy Sacrifice during the week.

Do not dishonor the Catholicity of your house by having un-Catholic and disedifying socials and drinking-parties in it, or even innocent amusements during Lent and other penitential times.

## BLESSINGS AND BLESSED ARTICLES.

The blessings of the Church are very numerous. They are given either directly to the faithful in person, to those who are sick, as well as to those who are in health; or they are imparted indirectly to them through objects which the Church blesses for that purpose.

## The Churching of Women.

One of the principal blessings of the Church, eagerly sought by Catholics, is that which is given to a mother after childbirth, called churching.

The mother is not bound to receive this blessing and consequently does not commit a sin, if she neglects it. It is a free blessing or private devotion.

The receiving of this blessing supposes a mother's first visit to the Church after her happy deliverance. It may be received, however, also later on according to convenience. It is also an act of thanksgiving on the part of the mother. But, there is little object in asking for this blessing after a long time, if one has neglected it in the beginning.

It is customary for such mothers to make an offering on this occasion. It is usual to offer a wax candle for the altar, or the price of the same.

In many cases the mother brings the

child with her to the church, but this is not necessary.

As this ceremony of churching supposes the mother's visit to be her first, or her introduction to the church after her confinement, it is customary in some places for her to kneel at the church-door, or in the rear of the church with a lighted candle in her hand. Otherwise she should kneel at the altar-rail for the whole ceremony.

When the Priest offers the end of his stole to her to be kissed, she should take it with her right hand, and devoutly press it to her lips, holding the candle in her left hand.

If she has knelt in the rear of the church, she rises then and follows the Priest to the altar-rail where she kneels again and receives his final blessing, making the sign of the cross on herself.

She finally delivers the candle to the server, and the price of it also, if it had been loaned to her from the vestry; and remains some minutes in thanksgiving, praying especially for her child.

## Blessed Candles.

EVERY Catholic household should be provided with one or more blessed candles. These candles should be of pure bees' wax. Other kinds, such as parafine, spermaceti or tallow candles will not answer the purpose of candles prescribed by the Church. It is well to procure the candles, therefore, either at the church or from a dealer in Catholic church goods.

Have the candles blessed on Candlemas Day, February 2, or at the regular time when articles of devotion are blessed in your church.

Have a pair of candlesticks for them, so as to be able to light them at once when they are needed.

They are needed particularly when Holy Communion or the last sacraments are administered, as well as at a funeral. It is well to light them also in times of great distress, as in sudden dangerous sickness, on occasions of violent storms, fires, floods, and the like; as the candles convey a blessing to the house.

## Imposition of the Ashes.

As Holy Church opens the penitential season of Lent by the blessing of ashes and by placing them on the heads of the faithful, all good Catholics ought to go to church on that day, although it is not of precept, and be reminded by this sacred ceremony of the certainty of death and of the necessity of preparing for it by Christian penance and mortification.

Unless by chance a person's face has been considerably besmirched by the dropping of the ashes, these ought not to be removed afterwards; but should be left to remain for the day at least, as a reminder of the holy season of penance and as a profession of faith.

As the ashes must be imposed by the Priest and are blessed only for that purpose, there is no object in taking them home.

The words pronounced by the Priest in placing the ashes on the head, are, "Remember, man, thou art dust, and unto dust thou wilt return."

## Blessed Palm.

THE palm which the Church blesses on Palm Sunday is another means by which she conveys her blessings to the homes of the faithful.

The blessed palm should be hung in conspicuous places in the house, usually placed over a crucifix or sacred picture. Some of it may be burned in times of great calamities, to avert the anger of God and secure His blessing and protection.

It should be burned previously to receiving the new palm, and not thrown away. Blessed articles should not be thrown aside when no longer needed or of use, but should be destroyed, burned or buried.

## Easter Water.

EASTER water is the water blessed by the Church on Holy Saturday for the baptismal font. Before the holy oils are poured into the font, the Priest takes some of the water and sprinkles the congregation with it as on Sundays before the High Mass. Some more of it is taken for the holy water fonts in the church; also for sprinkling in the houses of the people, as well as for sprinkling the faithful in church on Easter Sunday before the High Mass.

As the Church does not mention the use of Easter water outside of these occasions, it is not necessary to take a large quantity of it from the church, but a small vial of it is sufficient for the sprinkling of the house and its members on Holy Saturday and on Easter Sunday.

It must not be used in the sick-room and for the ordinary blessings of the Church when holy water is prescribed, but holy water must be used on these occasions.

## Holy Water.

EVERY Catholic household should be provided with a vessel of holy water.

The supply of holy water, as becomes its sacred character, should be kept in a large, presentable bottle or cruet, but not in a liquor bottle, or in an open jar liable to gather dust and form an unclean sediment. Bottles made specially for holy water, are easily procured now-a-days, or at least large, glass-stoppered cologne bottles or cruets are easily obtained in the stores for a trifling sum.

Holy water should, moreover, be kept in fonts hung on the wall or door-frame in the principal rooms, especially in the bedrooms that the members of the family may sign or sprinkle themselves with it occasionally, especially on retiring at night and on rising in the morning.

Holy water, both in church and at home, should not be used for any other purpose, but that intended by the Church, namely, for blessings by means of sprinkling. Any other use of it is more or less an abuse, which sometimes becomes even disgusting. It should never be used as a drink.

## Articles of Devotion.

ALL good Catholics should possess certain articles of devotion to which are attached special blessings and indulgences, such as a small crucifix, that can be worn on the person, a pair of beads, the scapulars, Agnus Deis, medals and the like.

They should have these articles blessed and indulgenced for their own personal use. Agnus Deis do not need to be blessed by the Priest, as they contain wax blessed by the Holy Father himself.

## THE PRINCIPAL DEVOTIONS.

### Vespers.

THE faithful should endeavor to assist at vespers, as this service is the one most recommended after Holy Mass.

As there are no prayers grander, more sublime and more devotional, than the holy psalms, the faithful should read them attentively at vespers, especially those which are sung by the choir, to which they should strive to conform, and which they should also endeavor to sing when the plain chant is employed.

The congregation should follow the Priest in his various postures at vespers, not the altar-boys. They should stand when he stands or walks, sit when he sits, bow when he bows and kneel also when he kneels.

## Benediction of the Blessed Sacrament.

No benediction of the Church should be coveted more than that of the Blessed Sacrament.

The faithful should kneel from the time the Blessed Sacrament is taken from the Tabernacle until it is put back again after the blessing with it has been given. They should remain in profound adoration of it all during the time of its exposition. No one should sit during benediction-service.

All should bow low and bless themselves when the Priest turns towards them and blesses them with the Sacred Host contained either in the monstrance or in the ciborium.

If anyone should enter or leave the church whilst the Blessed Sacrament is exposed for benediction, or before it has been put back into the tabernacle, he should genuflect profoundly with both knees bowing the head at the same time.

When the choir sings the psalm "Laudate Dominum" after the benediction and the tabernacle-door has been closed, the congregation should rise and remain standing until the Priest has left the sanctuary.

**Plenary Indulgences.**

MANY devotions and practices in the Church have the gaining of a plenary Indulgence attached to them. This indulgence can be gained, however, only by complying carefully with certain prescribed conditions.

The usual conditions prescribed for gaining a plenary indulgence are, to confess one's sins, to receive Holy Communion, to visit the church, and to pray for the intentions of the Holy Father.

To gain any indulgence, the soul must be in the state of grace. To be rid of the temporal punishment due to any particular sin, whether mortal or venial, such sin must be previously forgiven.

It is necessary to go to confession when confession is made an express condition for the gaining of an indulgence, although the soul be only in the state of venial sin. The confession may be made on the day preceding the day for which the indulgence is granted.

As for those who go weekly to confession and are in the habit of confessing venial sins, their weekly confession will suffice for them in order to gain all the plenary indulgences granted until their next confession, whether such confession be in the beginning or at the end of either week, provided they confess in each week.

Neither confession nor Communion need take place in any particular church, unless positively stated in the granting of the indulgence.

The visit required to the church may be made by receiving Holy Communion there, provided the condition of praying for the intentions of the Sovereign Pontiff be fulfilled at the same time.

If one is entitled to several plenary indulgences on the same day, however, as frequently happens on the part of those who practice many works of piety, it will be necessary both to visit the church and to pray for the intention of the Holy Father, as often on that day as one is entitled to gain a plenary indulgence.

As for those who are permanently disabled from visiting the church and receiving Holy Communion frequently, the Holy See has granted their confessors the faculties of substituting other good works instead.

The prayers required for the intentions of the Sovereign Pontiff may be any approved prayers of the Church and should be to the extent of at least five times the Our Father and Hail Mary.

In practicing any devotion to which plenary indulgences have been attached, it is necessary to make oneself familiar with the various occasions and conditions for gaining them, given in prayer books and special manuals published in connection with such devotions.

## The Rosary.

EVERY Catholic should have a rosary or pair of beads. The rosary is blessed and indulgenced for a person's own use by a Priest having the necessary faculties.

If a rosary thus blessed and indulgenced is transferred to another, the indulgence is lost, and the rosary must be blessed and indulgenced again. If a rosary, however, is merely loaned to another for use, without any intention to transfer the indulgence, the indulgence is not lost to the owner.

When a rosary is repaired and some new portions are substituted for the old ones, the rosary does not lose its blessing and indulgences.

Although the complete rosary consists of fifteen decades, five decades, however, or a chaplet, as it is called, are usually recited at a time. Each decade consists of one Our Father, ten Hail Marys, and the Glory be to the Father. The recitation of the decades is usually preceded by the Apostles' Creed, one Our Father, three Hail Marys, for an increase of faith, hope and charity, with a Glory be to the Father, both after the Creed and after the three Hail Marys.

To gain the indulgences granted for the devout recitation of the rosary, the faithful must endeavor to meditate on the mysteries of the rosary.

The mysteries of the rosary are: I. The Five Joyful Mysteries; 1. The Annunciation, 2. The Visitation, 3. The Nativity of Our Lord, 4. The Presentation of Our Lord in the Temple, 5. The Finding of Our Lord in the Temple. II. The Sorrowful Mysteries; 1. The Agony in the Garden, 2. The Scourging at the Pillar, 3. The Crowning with Thorns, 4. The Carrying of the Cross, 5. The Crucifixion. III. The Glorious Mysteries; 1. The Resurrection, 2. The Ascension, 3. The Sending of the

Holy Ghost, 4. The Assumption of Our Lady into Heaven, 5. The Coronation of Our Lady in Heaven.

All Catholics should make themselves familiar with the mysteries of the rosary by frequently reading of them in the Gospels and in devotional works.

Those who cannot possibly meditate on the mysteries, can gain the indulgences by simply reciting the prayers.

Most prayer-books point out the manner of reciting the rosary, containing also short meditations on the mysteries. They give also various introductory and closing prayers in connection with the essential part of the rosary.

Another condition for gaining the indulgences granted for the recitation of the rosary, requires that the beads be held in the hands whilst saying them. If several, however, say the beads in common, it will suffice if the leader complies with this condition.

## The Scapular.

There are various scapulars in use. The oldest and more common one, however, worn by the faithful, is that of our Lady of Mt. Carmel known as the Brown Scapular. It consists of two pieces of brown woolen cloth, worn respectively on the breast and on the back, connected over each shoulder with a piece of tape. It is an imitation and abbreviation of the large scapular or garment worn by the Carmelites. It is at the same time a badge of honor to the Mother of God, who revealed the devotion to the Carmelite Order in the person of St. Simon Stock.

The spiritual advantages of the scapular are, among many, the special protection of the Blessed Virgin, a share in the merits of all the good works performed by the Carmelites, and many indulgences, plenary and partial.

Neither the wearing of the scapular, even if one has been enrolled in it, nor the recitation of the prayers connected with it, bind under pain of sin. Hence, any neglect in this respect should not be made a matter of confession.

If this brown scapular becomes worn out or is lost, it is not necessary to have a new one blessed or to be enrolled again. The blessing of the old scapular is transferred to the new one without any ceremony.

Each one desiring to wear a scapular must be enrolled personally by a priest having the necessary faculties. No one can have another enrolled by simply bringing a pair of scapulars to the Priest to have them blessed for such a one.

Taking the scapular off when necessary, to replace it as soon as convenient, does not deprive the wearer of its benefits.

Neglecting to wear it for some time, however, although one does not need to be enrolled again in order to resume it, deprives, nevertheless, of its spiritual advantages during such time.

If the scapular, on the other hand, has been laid aside purposely, with the intention of abandoning it, a new enrollment in it would be necessary, in order to wear it with benefit again.

Plenary indulgences granted to wearers of the Brown Scapular may be gained on the following occasions under the usual conditions for gaining such indulgences:

On the day of enrolment, on the Feast of Our Lady of Mount Carmel, (July 16), or on the following Sunday, or on any day within the octave; on the feasts of the Immaculate Conception, Nativity, Presentation, Annunciation, Visitation, Purification, and Assumption of Our Blessed Lady; also on the feasts of St Joseph, St. Simon Stock, (May 16), St. Ann, St. Michael, St. Teresa and on any Wednesday of the year.

See Plenary Indulgences, page 179.

For the gaining of other indulgences, plenary and partial, see special manuals, published on the scapulars.

## The Way of the Cross,

THE beautiful devotion of the "Way of the Cross" or "Stations of the Cross," as it is variously called, is represented in most churches by the fourteen pictures of Our Lord's passion, or crosses found in them. Most prayer-books contain suitable meditations for this devotion.

What is essentially necessary in making the way of the cross, is to move from station to station, and to make a shor reflection on the sufferings of our Lord before each one of them.

But when this devotion is performed in public, it will suffice for the priest and his assistants to make the journey from station to station, whilst the others remain at their places.

It is well to make an act of contrition before beginning the way of the cross.

To gain the indulgences attached to the way of the cross at least five "Our Fathers," five "Hail Marys" and the "Glory be to the Father" should be said at the end of the devotion for the intention of the Sovereign Pontiff.

As for the sick and for those who are otherwise physically disabled from going to church to make the way of the cross, a small crucifix may be specially indulgenced for them by such as have the necessary faculties. By holding this crucifix in the hand and reciting twenty times each the " Our Father," " Hail Mary " and " Glory be to the Father " before it, all the indulgences granted in favor of the way of the cross, may be gained.

### The Forty Hours' Adoration.

THIS devotion performed in most churches once in the year, is designed to kindle in the faithful great love and reverence for the Most Blessed Sacrament as well as to make reparation to our Dear Saviour in the sacrament of His Love for so much coldness, indifference and such great outrages committed against Him by so many ungrateful beings.

It is the custom of all fervent Catholics to approach the sacraments on this occasion and visit the Blessed Sacrament exposed on the altar during the days of the devotion.

To encourage these practices the Sovereign Pontiffs have granted a plenary indulgence to all the faithful who confess their sins, receive Holy Communion and visiting the church during the adoration, pray for the Sovereign Pontiffs' intentions.

The confession may be made previously to the opening of the devotion, as on the day before it, or in the case of weekly penitents, at their usual time.

The Communion may be received on the morning of the day on which the devotion is opened, although the opening has not yet taken place. It is, moreover, not necessary, that the Communion be received in the church where the adoration is held.

To gain the plenary indulgence of the Forty Hours' Devotion it is necessary to visit the church during the adoration.

Besides the plenary indulgence, a partial indulgence of ten years and ten quadragenes is granted for each visit made to the Blessed Sacrament exposed during this devotion. All these indulgences are applicable to the souls in Purgatory.

The faithful, according to the desire of the Church, should endeavor to visit the church on each of the days and spend some time in adoration. They should, moreover, bring candles, flowers and other ornaments for the decoration of the altar, or contribute in money for the same. They should show the liveliest interest and exhibit the greatest fervor on this occasion, as one of the best to exercise their faith and piety.

## Novenas.

A NOVENA is a devotion ordinarily of nine days, made either as a preparation for some feast, or made at any time usually for the purpose of obtaining some favor.

Novenas made as a preparation for a feast, are made during the nine days preceding the feast day, so that the feast day itself would be the tenth day from the beginning of the novena.

There are many devotions for novenas found in the prayer-books. When no special devotion is prescribed, or if one does not choose to follow a prescribed devotion, it is customary to say at least nine Hail Marys on each of the nine days. There is no limit to the other prayers and practices that may be performed on these days. Individual fervor must suggest most of them.

There is nothing of obligation or of special precept in the making of novenas. It is well, however, to confess at the beginning of a novena, especially if one should be in sin. It is customary, also, to receive Holy Communion on the morning following the Novena, that is, on the feast-day, or on the tenth day.

Other devotions and practices suitable in making novenas are, for instance, the hearing of Holy Mass, having Masses said, visits to the church, fasting, abstaining, almsgiving, offerings made to the Church, prudent promises, especially when directed by the Confessor. and many other acts of piety and self-denial, suggested by individual devotion and fervor.

## PIOUS ORGANIZATIONS IN THE PARISH.

EVERY Catholic having at heart both his own salvation and sanctification, as well as the interests of his holy religion, should attach himself doubly to his Church by belonging to some special institution connected with it.

Every parish possesses one or more of these institutions, known as societies, sodalities, confraternities, or the like.

If a society is a beneficial organization only, having a Catholic name and enjoying the patronage of the Church, but requiring of its members no further practice of religion than is enjoined upon all Catholics, the members of such societies ought also to belong to some other organization in the parish, which is more intimately connected with the Church by its practice of special piety.

It is not good to join too many organizations, lest one only neglect his duties in them. Whatever organization a Catholic may belong to, and the more so, if he be an officer in it, he ought to cherish the same and take the liveliest interest in its affairs. He ought to observe its rules scrupulously and attend its meetings punctually. Whoever cannot do this, especially if he is charged with the important affairs of the association, ought rather to resign and not injure the good work by his neglect.

Anyone requested to resign his office for such reasons, ought not to take offense, but ought rather tender his resignation with good grace and take a subordinate position.

For the success of any pious organization not offering pecuniary or temporal benefit of any kind to its members, is required, above all other requisites, the practice of constant charity, self-sacrifice, mutual forbearance and humility. Without the practice of these virtues on the part of members, the best and largest church-organizations soon go to pieces. One must sacrifice himself for the general good, bearing misunderstandings, humiliations, even affronts from members, officials, if not from the directors themselves.

The primary object to be sought always and ever in Catholic organizations, must not be one's own pleasure, popularity or temporal advantage, but the honor of God, the sanctification of the soul and the good of our neighbor.

To leave off a good work solely because one has been offended or inconvenienced, when all the above-mentioned objects can be obtained by one's perseverance in it, is bad grace, weak faith and want of charity.

The following are some of the more popular and practical parish-organizations that exist in this country.

**League of the Sacred Heart of Jesus.** This is one of the grandest, and at the same time easiest and most practical organizations of piety at present in vogue in the Church. It is at the same time a kind of confraternity of the **Living Rosary** and a grand **Apostleship of Prayer.**

**The Third Order of St. Francis.** This is a branch of the great religious order of St. Francis, established by the holy Founder of the Franciscans himself in favor of lay people who wish to share the advantages of the Franciscan Order, without abandoning their respective state of life in the world. Members are enrolled in it by the Franciscan Fathers or others duly delegated by them. Besides greatly encouraging a life of higher perfection, the good works performed through it are rewarded with many indulgences and other spiritual advantages.

**The Archconfraternity of the Holy Family.** This organization exists in many parishes, there being meetings at stated times for all the members of the parish according to their sex and state, at which meetings instructions are given suitable to the different states of life, and various devotions are performed and good works encouraged.

**The Association of Christian Families,** lately instituted by Our Holy Father, Pope Leo XIII, to honor the Holy Family of Nazareth, exists in most parishes.

**The Holy Name Society.** This society is very popular among Catholic men and youths particularly. It is designed to encourage great reverence for the Holy name of God and of our Blessed Redeemer; as well as to make reparation for the abuse given the name of God by the profanation of it so common at the present time.

**The Society of Christian Mothers,** as its name would indicate, is intended for the instruction and encouragement of the married women of the parish in all things conducing to the true welfare of the Christian family.

**The Sodality of the Living Rosary.** By the practices of this sodality, the frequent recitation of the rosary, and a powerful form of prayer is secured. The members recite a decade of the beads each day, the mystery of which is assigned to them each month, together with the exercise of some particular virtue, and the honoring of a monthly Patron Saint.

**The Sodality of the Children of Mary** for young women is an admirable institution in a parish for keeping young women together, for preserving them from the dangers common to their state of life, and for encouraging them in the regular and fervent practice of their holy religion. The members usually interest themselves in various good works connected with the parish.

**The Altar-Society** is an institution in many parishes in which the women principally interest themselves in the care and adornment of the altar and sanctuary. By the regular payment of a trifling sum on the part of the members, much may be accomplished towards the decoration and well-keeping of the altars and sanctuary, even in the poorest parishes. The members should be willing also to give their personal services when required.

**The Conference of St. Vincent de Paul,** consisting of able and influential men of the parish in co-operation with the Pastor for the relief of poverty and suffering among the members of the parish, is calculated to relieve all deserving poverty that may exist in the average parish, as well as to aid the Pastor in his efforts in behalf of the temporal and moral welfare of his people. It is at the same time a splendid testimonial of the genuine Catholicity and charity of the men of the parish.

**Temperance and Abstinence Societies** are a necessity in the average parish, especially in large cities. They should be maintained not only for those who through weakness must abstain from intoxicating drinks, but should be patronized equally by those who are fond of a drink without the danger of abusing it. We should practice abstinence for the sake of self-denial to encourage the weak by our example. The example of Catholics in general in this respect, is calculated to do more good than prohibition and some other temperance movements.

Other Catholic organizations too numerous to mention in this small work, existing in various localities, according to the needs of Catholic people, ought to be patronized in preference to secular organizations of a purely beneficial or social character.

## CONDUCT TOWARDS THE PASTOR AND OTHERS OF THE CLERGY.

CATHOLICS should look upon their Pastor as their common father. As children are bound to love, obey and respect their parents, so must Catholics behave towards him whom God has placed over them to watch, to care for and to guide their souls. As much as the immortal soul is above the perishable body, so much greater must be the reverence of Catholics for their spiritual father.

When meeting him they must always recognize him. Only in the presence of the Blessed Sacrament must they omit their usual recognition of him. In the vestry, in the porch of the church, about its premises, in the school, they must greet him, rise at his approach, if they are sitting, and generally discontinue their occupation until he has passed them or bidden them to resume their former position or employment.

Men and boys meeting him on the street, or in public places, should always raise their hats or bow their heads to him. When passing very close to him, they should also bid him the time of the day.

Women meeting him on the street or in public places, especially when close to him, should always recognize him by a slight bow of the head and by a salutation in a low tone of voice.

Men should always offer their seat to the Priest in the cars, especially when they are close to him.

Catholics should not be offended if the Priest does not always return their greeting. In some places where Catholics invariably greet the Priest, he becomes so accustomed to it, that he does not always notice it. Sometimes the number of persons that salute him, is so great that it becomes impossible for him to notice each individual. At other times he is engaged in prayer, especially when going to the sick or when carrying the Blessed Sacrament. In the latter case he purposely abstains from returning their salutations, receiving their respect not to himself, but to the Blessed Sacrament, which he carries on his breast.

When you know that the Priest is carrying the Holy Eucharist to the sick, show the greatest reverence, but do not bid him the time of the day or speak to him.

If you meet him in or about the church or house on that sacred errand, fall on your knees at once and remain kneeling until he has passed; if on the street, step aside and bow with great reverence.

When the Priest comes to your house, do not try to avoid him, but let all who are in a condition for it, strive to meet him and at least exchange a few words with him. If he visits the family at large, let all endeavor to honor him by their presence.

Many Catholics have the devout practice of asking the Priest's blessing before he leaves the house, in which case all present kneel for it.

In calling upon the Priest, be sure that you call at a suitable time. Try to know the Priest's hours for receiving callers and for transacting parochial business.

Do not molest the Priest with unnecessary calls. Remember his time is usually more taken up with a multiplicity of occupations than that of any other professional man. His time is seldom his own. The average Priest has scarcely time to attend to all the onerous duties of his sacred calling, as well as answer all the calls made upon him. Between his Mass and breviary, other prayers and spiritual exercises, his confessions, sick calls and spiritual ministrations, his care of the church and its appurtenances, his business affairs, his superintendence of the school, his visits to the poor and needy of his parish, his study, reading and preparation of sermons, his activity in general church-affairs and neighboring institutions, his meals, rest and necessary relaxation, his attention to business-men, agents and professional callers, his courtesy to his parishioners, friends and benefactors, and a hundred other occupations; the Priest would almost need a day doubly as long as the present one of twenty-four hours.

Do not interrupt the Priest at his devotions, especially at his thanksgiving after Mass. Never speak to him immediately after Mass unless it is positively unavoidable and then only after a proper excuse. The Priest must then, above all times, attend to prayer after the most sacred function of his priesthood.

It is greatly to be regretted that this is the only time some people can find to confer with the priest. In most cases they could, at least, wait a little while or come at some more suitable time.

Persons desiring Holy Communion, however, after Mass or some blessing either for themselves or for some article of devotion, should approach the Priest before he removes the sacred vesments, that he may not be compelled to vest himself again or to put off the applicants to some other time.

Do not trouble the Priest with business-schemes. Do not think that because you are a member of his congregation and contribute to his support and to the support of religion, that, therefore, he and the Church must patronize your business. This is making a business out of religion. The Pastor and the Church exist for the sole purpose of religion. Business with them is entirely accidental and must not, therefore, interfere with religion or the obligation to support it.

Do not endeavor to borrow money from the Priest. This always puts him into a very embarrassing position. The Priest, it is true, must be all charity towards his people; but to take advantage of this his position as a kind father, is bad policy. It is frequently the cause of dissatisfaction, abuse and even of scandal. Experience teaches that few who borrow money from the clergy, ever return it. Remember the money that a priest loans is his own money. He dare not lend money that belongs to the church.

Catholics should remember that most Priests have nothing, because they are always giving and lending money. It is a shame to take the little cash they may have on hand. Some few of them have a little money because they have prudently saved it. It is not right to deprive them of it.

Never come to the Priest to complain about your neighbor, merely for the sake of getting satisfaction, when some unpleasantness has occurred and nothing can be done about it. Only in the case of an abuse going on, which it is the Pastor's business to remove, or to know of, let it be your duty to report it to him.

Be not quick to report the conduct of others to the Priest, unless you know he desires the information.

Do not expect the priest to do your own unpleasant work of reprimanding the members of your family, when you have not the courage to do it yourself. When engaging the services of a Priest to correct anyone, do not take him or the guilty parties by surprise by underhand action in the matter. Do not exasperate parties by calling the Priest suddenly to them to reprimand them. Prepare them for it by repeated threats to that effect. Do not expect the Priest not to let on whence he has the knowledge of their conduct, when the source of that knowledge is evident.

Always be grateful to the Priest and thank him by word or deed, for every act of kindness he does you, and for the attention he gives you in your calls upon him.

Remember the spiritual favors he does you, cannot be compared to temporal favors. His ministrations are above earthly compensation. Do not begrudge him his meagre allowance for his services. Bear in mind that men of similar ability in other professions exact large fees for every single exercise of their profession. The Priest might have chosen a career like theirs and have acquired their usual wealth and comfort.

Do not be content with repaying his services with money only; but whenever convenient, offer also your services to him, and share with him those goods with which God may have blessed you.

Recognize in your Pastor the representative of God. Overlook his possible faults and remember that he too is a man.

Do not speak of his faults, but conceal them as much as you can. Unless we learn to bear one another's burdens, as one of the crosses of this life, we shall never be true Christians.

Always pray for your Pastor, particularly at Holy Mass, and when he is dead, insert his name in your daily prayers and have a Mass said for him occasionally.

If great reverence is due to Priests, still greater reverence must be shown to Bishops.

It is customary to kneel and receive his blessing when meeting a Bishop, kissing his ring at the same time, unless it be on the street or in some public place.

When the faithful receive Holy Communion from the Bishop, they kiss his ring as soon as he approaches them.

The following are the ordinary titles and the manner of addressing the Clergy:

For a Priest: Your Reverence; Rev. N. N., Rev. dear sir, or Rev. dear Father.

For a Bishop: Your Lordship; Right Rev. N. N., D. D. (Doctor of Divinity); Right Rev. dear sir, or Right Rev. dear Bishop.

For an Archbishop: Your Grace; Most Rev. N. N., D. D., Most Rev. dear sir, or Most Rev. dear Archbishop.

For a Cardinal: Your Eminence; Most Rev. N. N., D. D., Most Rev. dear sir, or Most Rev. dear Cardinal; Most Eminent dear sir, or Most Eminent dear Cardinal.

www.ingramcontent.com/pod-product-compliance
Lightning Source LLC
Chambersburg PA
CBHW031817220426
43662CB00007B/693